Light Atonement

by
Ariyana
~ a star child ~

PROSPECTA PRESS

WESTPORT, CONNECTICUT 2015

Light Atonement copyright © 2015 by Ariyana ~a star child~ LLC.

All rights reserved. No portion of this book may be reproduced in any fashion, print, facsimile, or electronic, or by any method yet to be developed, without express written permission of the publisher.

Published by
Prospecta Press
An imprint of Easton Studio Press
P.O. Box 3131
Westport, CT 06880
(203) 571-0781
www.prospectapress.com

10 9 8 7 6 5 4 3 2 1

Book and cover design by Barbara Aronica-Buck (www.bookdesigner.com)
Cover art by Deborah DeLisi (www.delisiart.com)
Author photo by Hernan Rodriguez (www.hernanphotography.com)

Hardcover ISBN: 978-1-63226-028-4
Paperback ISBN: 978-1-63226-029-1
E-book ISBN: 978-1-63226-030-7

First edition

Manufactured in the United States of America
First printing March 2015

For Humankind:

May you realize who you are,

may you feel love deeply in this lifetime,

and may this book help you awaken.

CONTENTS

PREFACE - VII

PART I ~ PAST ~ 1

CHAPTER 1:
The Hammered Nail: My Childhood in Japan ~ 3

CHAPTER 2:
Following Your Inner Voice ~ 13

CHAPTER 3:
Soul Searching ~ 23

CHAPTER 4:
Taking Responsibility for Your Actions ~ 37

CHAPTER 5:
Unfinished Business ~ 45

PART II ~ JOURNEY: WITHIN AND BEYOND ~ 53

CHAPTER 6:
Spiritual Growth ~ 55

CHAPTER 7:
Awakening ~ 75

CHAPTER 8:
Language of Light ~ 95

CHAPTER 9:
Waiting for the Green Light ~ 113

CHAPTER 10:
My Life's Purpose ~ 129

CHAPTER 11:
Facing My Destiny ~ 139

CHAPTER 12:
Coming Home ~ 151

PART III ~ FUTURE ~ 171

CHAPTER 13:
Walking Your Path Without Judgment ~ 173

CHAPTER 14:
My Dreams, Wishes, and Hopes ~ 189

CHAPTER 15:
My Questions ~ 197

ACKNOWLEDGEMENTS ~ 207

ABOUT THE AUTHOR ~ 209

PREFACE

All of us who are here on Earth came with purpose and commitment. When my inner voice said, "It is time for you to quit the furniture business and to do what you came here for," I had no choice but to follow that voice. This book is about my life's journey, my search to find who I am, why I am here, and what I am going to do. I was living a Cinderella story. By age 30, I had everything most people dream of having. I came from Japan as a teenager to live in the United States, built a very successful business as a young adult, and then had beautiful children. From anyone's viewpoint, I had it made. But, deep inside, I felt something was missing. There had to be more to life than material success, family, and work. Then I started searching. Once I started my spiritual journey, my search got deeper and deeper, and my realizations became greater and greater.

I began by addressing my emotional state with the Hoffman Institute, learned how to work with energy using the Reiki method, and connected to my source by learning to meditate with Vipassanā Buddhism. Then I was drawn to psychics and healing powers. I worked with crystals and healers and visited many powerful energy vortices, such as Sedona and Mount Shasta.

My spiritual journey wasn't always easy, and my experiences over the last several years have defied logic, practical nature, and everything I believed to be true. However, I knew deeply that there is a reason for everything and that my journey would take me somewhere I needed to go.

I first encountered my star family (Angels) from other dimensions while meditating in Mount Shasta a few years ago. I didn't understand the true meaning at that time, but I felt in my heart that what they were saying was true, and they told me that they were my family and they loved me. Then that led to my biggest surprise of my life when I started to speak light languages. My star family started speaking through me to bring messages for humanity.

They revealed that I had been chosen to communicate great truths and that people need to hear them. That humans and Earth are going in the wrong direction and I am here to lead them to the brighter future. I know some of you are wondering how this is possible or doubting what I am telling you. How can one person make such a huge difference? I understand that. Because I felt the same way and asked that question again and again to my angels and other beings who speak through me.

I wrote my life story chronologically in this book. After each chapter, I created a reflection section so you too can look back at your life and start your own journey. I included some meditations so that those of you who want to learn how to meditate can do so. Throughout this book, you'll also find italicized sections describing dreams shown to me by my angels based on actual events I experienced in the past.

All I am asking of you is to be open-minded as you read my story; then decide what you believe when you are done with the book. I am writing this book not because I want to be famous or want money. I am writing it because the act of writing and telling my story is part of my life purpose.

> With love and light,
> Ariyana
> *December 17, 2014 in Los Angeles*

Something startled me as I awoke. I was unfamiliar with the room I was in. As I looked around, I saw sheer white linen curtains flowing in the wind. I heard the door burst open. Four men came in, all dressed in ornate clothing. They took me from my bed and pushed me into the dark corridor. Next thing I knew, I was in a dim, candlelit space, and I could smell incense burning—frankincense and myrrh. I bumped into a sarcophagus. Then I noticed that there were two sarcophagi: one sealed and the other empty. There was an older man standing at the opening. In his right hand he held a carved cane with the eye of a horse at the center of it. He was dousing some kind of liquid toward me with his left hand. Could it be holy water? I wondered. I was panting. Where was I? The older man left the room. Then the four elaborately clad men closed the entrance to the room with a stone. What was happening? There was nothing but darkness now. I couldn't breathe. Someone help me! I am dying in here. My ethereal body departed my corporeal body and began to float up toward the sky. Before I knew it, all the darkness turned into white light, and I could see three pyramids below me. Above me, I noticed three stars in the same formation, and three beams of white light between these and the pyramids. I was inside the three beams of light, rising up to the sky.

PART I

Past

CHAPTER 1

The Hammered Nail: My Childhood in Japan

It is not what you do for your children, but what you have taught them to do for themselves, that will make them successful human beings. –Ann Landers

I was born on August 5, 1971 in Tokyo, Japan, into an average, upper-middle class family, and I had a normal, peaceful upbringing. My father owned a small textile business, and my mother was a swimming teacher. I grew up with two sisters and a brother. Like most families in Japan, ours was very close. Even today, except for me, all my family members live within a 10-minute walk of one another. When I recall my childhood, I have many fond memories. Because we lived in a big metropolitan city, without much nature to speak of, we would get away from Tokyo whenever we could. In Japan there are four seasons. The cherry trees blossom in the warm spring, followed by an extremely hot and humid summer. The cool fall brings amazing colors in the foliage before the cold and wet winter sets in. The rural areas of Japan are beautiful—serene and mysterious. In the summers we would journey to the beaches and rivers, and we'd go to the hot springs in winter. I remember one summer night on a ferry, coming back from a family vacation in Hokkaido. I was very sad, crying, "I don't want to grow up—then we will have to go our separate ways."

When I was young, I also spent a lot of time with my extended family—great-grandmother, grandmother, uncle, and aunt on my mother's side. I felt very close to all of them. During our weekly visits, my aunt would make me sit in front of her Buddhist altar, and say hello to our ancestors. She was the most religious person in our family, often chanting for hours in front of that altar. Whenever I visited my relatives' home, they would make me or my siblings offer food—often snacks or fruit—placing it in front of the shrine. In Japan, we believe that our ancestors are watching over and protecting us.

When I was a child, my great-grandmother was in her late 80s, and, though she didn't speak much, I felt very comfortable being with her. Both my great-grandmother and grandmother were very quiet, but even then I could feel their inner strength. Many Japanese women are, in fact, much stronger inside than their petite and fragile outward appearance. They were unlike my aunt and uncle, who were very strict and made me change from using my left hand to my right, explaining that they didn't want me to be ashamed of this deviation when I grew up. Still, I found ways of being close to them too. My uncle loved to tell his war stories, and of how he and my aunt met. I would often just sit there for hours, playing shogi—Japanese chess—with him, listening to the same stories again and again.

When I was five years old, my great-grandmother passed away. In Japan, funerals are held for the entire neighborhood, making them a regular part of life that occurs almost every weekend. But my great-grandmother was the first whom I knew. It felt very strange to see her motionless and pale, lying on the bed in a white kimono. At her funeral, her body was cremated. Before the cremation, I saw her body whole. And when the box was opened afterwards, I saw only bones and ashes. In Japan, relatives of the deceased use chopsticks to collect the bones into a small box. The box is then placed in a family tomb, where all one's ancestors may rest their bones and ashes. I remember crying hysterically in my mother's arms that night, saying that I didn't want to be cremated when I died. I was frightened that I would be burnt alive.

My mother was my hero, and I wanted to be just like her when I grew up. She was Superwoman to me—she not only worked as a swimming teacher but also managed all the household chores and was an amazing cook. I don't know how she found time, but she often baked cakes when I came back from school, made dresses for my sisters and me, and played sports at my elementary school. In Japan it is common for schools to have teams for mothers, and mine was a star volleyball and table tennis player. She was also president of the PTA, and I felt quite proud of her as I watched her give speeches at school events.

My mother never met her father. He was sent to fight in

World War II three months after he married my grandmother. While he was deployed, my grandmother realized that she was pregnant with my mother, but my grandfather never returned. If you met my mother, you would never guess she was raised without a father. She is like a sun: warm, strong, and a beacon of light that people gravitate toward. Growing up, she swam competitively, and held a Japanese record for butterfly when she was in high school. I know she could achieve this amazing accomplishment only because she had trained extremely hard for many, many years. My mother taught us that we could accomplish anything through hard work, and I learned determination and confidence from her.

I was a very good student, and excelled at many sports. In Japan, four siblings is considered a large family, and I always thought I would be loved more and get more attention if I achieved excellence in everything I did. I started swimming competitively at the age of five, moved on to synchronized swimming when I was nine, and at the age of 11 was elected to the team representing Tokyo in the Japanese Junior Olympics. At that early age, I already knew never to give up if I wanted something. I also learned that things didn't always come easily but that your effort will pay off one way or another, and you must believe in yourself.

In order to get into a good school in Japan in the 1980s, one had to do well on their entrance exams. Fortunately, I performed well and was accepted by all the schools I applied to. I chose an all-girls institution in central Tokyo, which my older sister attended. I found school boring, but my whole world changed when I was introduced to what we in Japan call "Western Music." Duran Duran, Culture Club, Wham!, and Madonna were big hits. I started watching American films, and I absolutely fell in love with the way of life represented in them. It seemed to me that American culture was the opposite of Japanese. It was bigger and grander, and anything was possible. I asked my parents if I could study overseas in a Western high school, but my mother insisted that I finish high school in Japan.

I knew that in order to get into U.S. universities, my grades mattered, so I started to take school seriously. Once I put my energy into it, I earned straight A's, and I started to enjoy learning. I also spent summers in America, studying English. I knew that I wanted to live in the United States and didn't even think about applying for college in Japan, but I was glad my mother had insisted that I stay in Japan to finish high school. Between the 10th and 12th grades, I grew so much as a person. In addition to having my first boyfriend, in 10th grade, I had the opportunity to learn and understand more about the Japanese way of life, and over the course of those three years, my views of Japan completely changed. Instead of simply wanting everything American, I came to see the beauty in both cultures, and to appreciate where I came from.

Looking back, I can see that being raised in Japan was quite a challenging experience for me. There are so many unspoken rules that I cannot imagine anyone living there as a foreigner. One might say "no, thank you," but it could mean "yes," depending on the situation. I was always more direct than many people in Japan and didn't understand why things had to be so complicated. In Japan it is essential to look good in front of others. When children do something wrong, parents say: "Stop that. You're making me ashamed." Or even: "People are laughing at you." From the beginning I was different from my friends. I didn't care about what others thought of me, and I knew I didn't want to tell my children that they needed to behave in a certain way in order to save face.

Japanese religious beliefs are confusing as well. Except for a small percentage of the population who practice regularly, most Japanese people have very little interest in religion. They might bring a baby to a temple in order to celebrate when he or she is born, or visit shrines for a New Year's prayer. They might get married in a Christian church and have a funeral at a temple. My father claimed he was a Shingon follower (one of the sects of Buddhism), and my mother is a Jōdo Shinshū Buddhist; though when I was a teenager, I never saw them do anything religious. But having no strong religious preferences does not mean that Japanese people are less spiritual. They deeply understand the cycle of life, with birth and death close to their hearts. Perhaps the distinction to make is that Japanese people are spiritual rather than religious. In Japan, people seek truth within themselves, not from the outside or traditional religion. People are more connected to nature—e.g., working with bonsai or enjoying the four seasons. People are grounded and centered.

Through my upbringing, I learned that there is much about Japanese culture to admire—strong family ties, respect for elders and their belief systems, and that one can accomplish so much more as a part of a whole. Japan has a long history, and we value and preserve the traditions from our past. I love the fact that I learned to be conscious of others, as we share a small country, small houses, and limited resources. I was taught to help others who were in need, and to be kind and polite to everyone, because that is the way of life in Japan. Everyone in Japan works diligently without complaining, and from this I had a strong work ethic instilled in me from a young age. And while the Japanese honor the past, they do not dwell in it. The country has lost wars and has been affected by several natural disasters, but its people have never lost faith or hope, rebounding every time, no matter how difficult the road is. Growing up in Japan shaped who I am now. At the same time, however, I always felt that I was different, and that I didn't completely fit in. Being unique or authentic wasn't welcomed. "The nail which sticks up should be hammered down," as the Japanese saying goes. I never understood this concept. I also found myself resisting the male-oriented social framework, always protesting to my parents that my older brother received special treatment. Many people thought women shouldn't work, but instead serve their husbands and take care of their children. Even today, this is a sacrifice many Japanese women make. I knew from a very young age that that was not what I was going to do when I grew up. My parents weren't surprised when I chose to attend college in the United States. I never looked back.

Chapter 1 Reflections

We all have families, roots, and cultural backgrounds. Our childhood shapes who we are. However, we have the choice now to choose how we want to live and what we want to value and carry on from what we have learned as children. The past is gone, but remembering and appreciating your roots can stabilize your life and provide support.

Who are the three people who had the most positive influence in your childhood?

1._____

2._____

3._____

What are the three fondest memories from your childhood?

1._____

2._____

3._____
_____

What are the three most valuable lessons you learned from your childhood?

1._____
_____
2._____
_____
3._____
_____

Close your eyes, and take a deep breath. Open your eyes, and read the questions and the answers you have given. Take another deep breath, and feel the connection, love, and appreciation beyond yourself to your family, your roots, and your past.

CHAPTER 2

Following Your Inner Voice

*The most difficult thing is the decision to act.
The rest is merely tenacity.* – Amelia Earhart

When I was in high school, my dream was to become a businesswoman, flying around the world. I imagined catching a plane in my business suit, having a meeting in Hong Kong one day and Singapore the next. In order to realize this aspiration, I felt that I needed to leave Japan and become fluent in English. I was young and brave—or some may call it young and stupid—so when I was 18 years old, I left Japan to attend the University of Southern California.

When I arrived at USC, I was the only freshman who had come directly from a regular Japanese school. I had to take one English class for international students, but math and science came easily to me, and I managed to earn mostly A's in my first semester. School wasn't so difficult, but adjusting to life in an American college dorm was another matter.

Other than attending summer camp, I had never left home until that point. To compound the issue, the school had chosen another Japanese girl as my roommate, and she was quite mean. She was so mean, in fact, that she lost all her friends by the end of freshman year and never returned. Every day I called my mother, crying. She would reassure me and tell me not to worry, promising that it would get better. It wasn't until years later, after I had graduated from college, that my younger sister informed me that my mother would also cry after she hung up the phone.

In November of my freshman year, I was studying in one of the USC libraries when I saw a friend from history class, and we chatted for a few minutes. That same night, my friend called and said his roommate had seen me there and wanted to invite me to dinner. I had just turned 19, and Tim was 22. Less than a month after our first date, Tim and I became inseparable. Even though I'd had boyfriends before, I'd never known anyone who had such an intense interest in me. He would send me flowers and call throughout the day. And I'd always wanted to be wanted.

In my second year of college, I moved in with Tim. Everyone thought we were moving too fast, but I was young and didn't care what others thought. Tim was charismatic and charming, and most of all he wanted to be with me. I had never dated an American guy, so I thought everything he did was normal—like his road rage, or his fights with his parents that ended with them not speaking for months at a time, or how he barely attended class, scraping by with passing grades.

I suppose the old cliché "opposites attract" worked for us. Tim was different from anyone I knew, and different from me in many ways. He was interested in business, politics, and spirituality, and he loved to argue. My own debate skills, as well as my English, immediately improved as a result of fighting with him.

Tim was three years ahead of me at USC. He was just about to graduate when I was finishing my freshman year. He had studied entrepreneurship, which was a popular and demanding program at the USC School of Business. I continued to excel academically and decided to major in business as well. Tim's dream was to start his own company, and that dream came true when a friend of his returned from Indonesia and explained how he'd been purchasing furniture in a small village there and importing it to his hometown in Minnesota.

Tim went to see his friend's first shipment and fell in love with the idea of selling this furniture himself. It seemed like an easy business—buying a cabinet in Indonesia for $100 and selling it in the United States for $400. When Tim researched other importers, the prospect became even more promising. People were reselling similar pieces for around $1,500 wholesale. The big question became where to get the funds to purchase the first shipment.

My parents not only advanced us the $50,000 we needed to get started, but told us that we could keep and not pay back the money. It was the money they had saved for my marriage, and my mother urged us to get married before establishing our business together. So on my 21st birthday, we were wed in a Balinese temple in the town of Ubud. With our parents, my siblings, and our closest friends in attendance, our wedding was simple and warm.

At the start of the fall semester of my junior year, Tim and I received our first container of furniture. To our surprise, the pieces flew out of our storage space. We were selling beautiful, ornate, pieces of furniture—some of it very old—and, compared to our competitors, we sold it at bargain rates. We became an instant success. Instead of pricing our merchandise at a high profit margin, we chose to sell furniture at reasonable prices while moving a large volume. Tim soon envisioned expanding the company. We didn't have to make much per container, and we kept our costs low. I was still in school, and we were happy making a few thousand dollars a month

It was an exciting period, with our sales doubling and tripling each month. We were adding more warehouses and suppliers from more countries. Traveling to Asia in the early 1990s was incredible—the economy was booming everywhere we went. We visited Hong Kong, mainland China, Malaysia, Singapore, Thailand, India, the Philippines, and Vietnam, searching for furnishers.

By the time I graduated from USC in the summer of 1994, I was already working full-time, attending 20 trade shows a year and traveling 20 days out of each month. At the age of 22, I was running a successful business, managing several employees. At the age of 24, I was a millionaire. My sister Akiko moved to Los Angeles and joined our company. I was so happy to have her in my life again. Akiko and I had been best friends since we were young—we were like twins, sharing everything. She was the person whom I trusted most in the world.

But, even though I had my sister with me and material success, I knew something major was missing from my life. I decided to have children, and in 1998 my son was born. I will never forget the moment I held him, after 13 hours of labor. When I looked into his eyes, I felt like I was looking into myself. I had brought this little soul into the word, and I knew it was one of the most important things I would do in this life. Proud of myself, I felt new gratitude and appreciation for all mothers who had done this before me. I felt the urge to care for, love, and protect this child. I could just hold him in my arms and look into his eyes for hours at a time.

I never imagined that I could love someone so much. For the first time, I understood the true meaning of unconditional love and patience. Even though I was having a great time with my son, adjusting to my new lifestyle was difficult. I was a businesswoman, used to spending my days telling people what to do. Suddenly, I found myself up every night, breastfeeding and changing diapers. Tim wasn't so taken with parenting, and I felt like I was alone on my journey. My mother came for three months to help with the baby (and cook my favorite meals). Never having imagined that a child would be so much work, I hired a live-in nanny when my mother left. I often joked that if I had known what having a child entailed, I would have waited a few years.

In 2000, I was overjoyed to find out I was expecting a second child, a girl. I had always wanted a boy and a girl, and having both was truly a dream. With my daughter, I had a home birth, and it was one of the highlights of my life. She was born around 1:00 a.m., and afterwards, my son woke up and came into my room. I will never forget the expression on his face when he saw his little sister. He kissed us both, and then went back to his room. While I was pregnant with my daughter, I was worried, wondering how I could love her as much as I loved my son. But, when I held her in my arms, my love expanded beyond my imagination. For the first time, I knew that love was limitless. Yes, having my children completely changed my life and changed me as a human being.

Parenting is a difficult job. No one will pay you, nor will they praise you for what you do 24 hours a day, seven days a week. It is the hardest job on this Earth. But deep within myself I knew I was meant to be a mother, and that being one would give me the fulfillment my business could not. Having my children was a beautiful time in my life—just thinking about them still makes me smile. I've never laughed so much as when my children were little. It was, and is, such a joy to see them smiling and happy. And they loved me so much; they couldn't get enough of my attention. Whenever I was holding them, kissing them, or telling them how much I loved them, I knew I was healing *my* inner child.

Looking back, I'm struck by the way in which I adapted and evolved as circumstances changed. I am very lucky that I was born with the ability not to have unneeded fears or doubts. I always sensed that things would work out as they were supposed to and I did not need to go against the current. This deep knowledge gave me confidence and opened doors. Because I had no unnecessary fears or doubts, I saw my path clearly, and that made it easier to make the right choices. I also learned from a young age that you can attain any goals by working hard as long as they are the right goals for you. Since I knew what I wanted, I made the right moves and achieved my objectives. What helped me adapt and succeed, too, was my ability to let go when it was the right time and not to hang on to something that was no longer working. This way, my move to the United States, marrying an American guy, starting my business, and having children all represented a natural and clear evolution.

As you're about to discover, my ability to let go as well my lack of excessive fear and doubt enabled me to go on a journey that others may not have been willing to take.

Chapter 2 Reflections

We are terrified by fear. We are afraid of change, failure, social seclusion, and death. However, you cannot truly live if you let your fear control you and put you in a small box from which you cannot escape. You are in charge, and you can do anything you wish. Listen to your inner voice, which comes from your heart. Be gentle and patient with yourself. Recognize that you have spent years listening to your ego, which resides in your brain. It will take time before you can feel your heart and your heart's true longing. But know that it is your right to live from your heart.

What are the three important things you have accomplished that were out of your comfort zone?

1._____
_____

2._____
_____

3._____
_____

How did those three things make you feel?

1. _____
_____

2. _____
_____

3. _____
_____

What are the three things your heart says you love to do?

1. _____
_____

2. _____
_____

3. _____
_____

Close your eyes, and take a deep breath. Open your eyes, and read the questions and the answers you have given. Take another deep breath, and imagine that you are doing what your heart loves to do. Take another deep breath, close your eyes, and imagine how you feel while you are doing what your heart loves to do, and remember the feeling when you open your eyes.

CHAPTER 3

Soul Searching

If you want others to be happy, practice compassion. If you want to be happy, practice compassion. – Dalai Lama

My children were the center of my life, and I semi-retired from the business world. Tim and I were drifting apart, having difficulty getting our marriage to work. Having children definitely put a strain on our relationship—we had so much more work, different expectations, and less time for ourselves. No matter how many helpers I hired, I still had so much to do, and I wanted to give so much to our children. I was sacrificing myself—my life—and not taking good care of my own needs. Tim and I were fighting all the time. I felt as if I couldn't breathe, and I had no space of my own. I was miserable.

I had my first therapy session on my birthday in 2002. My therapist, Peggy, immediately saw that my heart was shut down and I wasn't letting anything or anybody in. Like most people, my heart had begun to shut down in childhood when I experienced pain. When I was in fifth grade, the school newspaper published an essay I wrote. I was proud of myself, but I came home to find my mom was very upset with me because I wrote about her pushing me to do well at school. I didn't receive the love and approval that I thought I deserved. It was this type of experience that made me close down a little at the time and feel that it wasn't safe to be completely open.

As I talked with Peggy, I came to understand that, emotionally, I was quite beaten up by being with someone like Tim, who was so loud and controlling, and who believed and said repeatedly that everything was my fault. I believed his words, and I was blaming myself for all that was passing between us.

I needed to find myself. Peggy suggested that I go to the Hoffman Institute and participate in their "Process." The Hoffman Institute Process is a week long personal development seminar. Peggy told me that by going to Hoffman for a week, I would cut the length of my therapy by two years. I couldn't imagine being in therapy for years to begin with. At that point, my least favorite thing to do was talk about my feelings. I was more comfortable keeping to myself, staying busy with my daily routines. Despite being in therapy, I didn't want to change, and I didn't want to face my problems. But I also knew that I couldn't keep pretending everything was OK. Something had to happen. I signed up for the Hoffman Process that day.

At the Hoffman Institute, they believe that everything we do—negative or positive—we learned from our parents, and that we can undo what we have learned and become whole as individuals. I didn't believe that spending a week in

Napa would change my personality, or my life, for the better. To my surprise, however, the Hoffman Process was a lifesaving experience for me. Over the course of the Process, I learned the ways in which I was living and acting just like my parents, or exactly opposite to them. I was expecting others to make me happy and save me. I was expecting too much from myself. I was very judgmental. The most important lesson I learned during my time at the Institute was to forgive myself, and to forgive others. I forgave my parents completely, as they were just doing their best. I forgave myself for all that was in my past. I didn't know the meaning of loving myself and others until I finished my Process. I had never cried so much in my life. I cried during the sessions, and I cried in my room at night. I hadn't known it was possible for me to feel so much. My heart, which had shut down a long time ago, completely reopened. On the last day of the Hoffman Process, I literally felt as though a cylinder of white light had opened up from my throat, moving down into my heart and to my stomach. Afterwards, I could finally feel my emotions and truly love myself and others. I felt hopeful for the first time, and I made a commitment to myself never to shut my heart down again. Learning the gift of forgiveness was my first step toward finding myself.

Coming back from the Hoffman Institute, and going back to my life, was difficult. I felt so much love and acceptance from the teachers and other friends who were a part of and attended the Process. But that is always the case with retreats: they create a safe space in which to do the work.

Then the real question becomes how to bring that safe space to our own homes, relationships, and lives. I kept listening to the CDs I received from Hoffman to remind myself that I was the center of my life, that I could create what I wanted to create, and that I had the ability to bring this into reality. That was the beginning of giving back to myself the power I had given away to others. I had no idea how long it would take for me to feel whole with nothing affecting me, but we all have to take the first step. I had already been practicing yoga for several years, but I began to attend classes with greater frequency and with greater intensity. I frequented more challenging sessions and made it a daily routine. I started to read books about self-improvement, meditation, and spirituality. I began to realize that I wasn't alone, and that many people were going through similar situations. I was lost, and I was searching. My life was on fire.

In order to help me cope with the changes in my life, Peggy introduced me to her Reiki master and suggested that I receive regular treatments. Reiki is a healing modality that was introduced from Japan by Mikao Usui. By simply "laying on hands," the Reiki practitioner causes unseen "life force energy" to flow to a client, which balances the client's "chi," or energy level. Reiki practitioners believe that if one's life force energy is low, one is more likely to get sick or feel stressed. When I received my first Reiki session, my entire body was humming, filled with warm energy. I felt whole, and I realized how depleted my chi had been. I couldn't believe that, just by having my master's hands on certain parts of my body, so much energy could run through me, making me feel complete and in harmony again. This was the first time I had ever experienced an energy healing session. I was hooked. I started seeing my Reiki master on a monthly basis for the next two years. In a few months' time, I signed up to take classes to become a Reiki practitioner myself. Somehow, I knew Reiki wouldn't be my career, but learning the techniques to heal myself and others—including my children—would certainly be useful. During class, we had the opportunity to send a distance healing to another student who was five feet away, lying flat on a massage table. I closed my eyes and concentrated on sending healing through my hands. After the session had finished, my teacher told me that a strong white light had come from my hands and shot toward the student on the table. My teacher thought I would be a powerful healer. I somehow knew that what my teacher was saying was true. I felt that Reiki came naturally to me and that I could heal with my energy.

Through Reiki classes, I learned about the chakra system, auras, unseen parts of the body and their surroundings, and how these all affect our physical, emotional, and light bodies. I also learned how important it is that all parts of our body, seen and unseen, be in harmony if we are to be truly whole and happy. This newfound understanding of the mystery of life and of the human body fascinated me.

Shortly after I completed the Hoffman Process, a friend suggested that I attend a silent meditation retreat at the Spirit Rock Meditation Center in Northern California. I had never meditated for more than 20 minutes in my life, but I leapt at the opportunity to spend 11 days away from home, and to be alone. I went on a Vipassanā meditation retreat. When I got there, I was stunned by the schedule! They would alternate 45 minutes of sitting meditation with 45 minutes of walking meditation. This would happen all day long, aside from meals, discussions with your teachers, working meditation, and the evening Dharma talks. Aside from the instructor discussions, which lasted for only 15 minutes, everything was conducted in complete silence. The first sitting started around 6:00 a.m., and the last sitting ended around 9:30 p.m.! To my surprise, I found not talking to be very comforting. I heard from teachers again and again that the hardest thing for most people is sitting, because of the physical discomfort, but as a result of my upbringing I had no body pain after a day of sitting meditation. I was quite lucky that I was from Japan, where we ate dinner on the floor and at low tables—I was already used to sitting on the ground with my spine straight. The chatter in my head, however, was another story. My mind kept telling story after story, over and over again, even though I was meditating in silence.

By the end of the fourth day, the chatter finally stopped. For the first time in my life, I was dwelling in complete silence. I was in a state of pure bliss, and I could feel warm energy vibrating throughout my body. The sensation was something I was very familiar with, and it was almost like I was coming home. You read about this kind of happening in books, but I was actually living it, and that was an incredible experience. Furthermore, I was drawn to all my teachers, who demonstrated so much peace, wisdom, and warmth. I am still very grateful that I first learned meditation in the Vipassanā tradition. Buddha taught that we all have compassion, that we need to live from our hearts, and that the highest good we can offer in this life is help to others. During one of my sitting sessions, I connected profoundly with the space of compassion I was carrying deeply within myself but hadn't known I possessed. As this happened, I cried and cried. I understood I was mother to myself, holding my inner child. For the first time, I was home, and I realized that everything I was looking for was already within me. Throughout my life, I had been looking for happiness outside myself and was never satisfied. But as I sat simply in silence, being with myself, I realized that I didn't need anything. I was happy, at peace, whole, and full of love for every sentient being on this Earth. I didn't want to leave the retreat. "How can I go back and live the same way?" I remember asking my teacher. "How can I be with my friends who don't know this?" My teacher replied that it was my dharma to live this way and to show others how to attain the same fulfillment through my example—there's no need to tell or change others unless they want to be taught and changed.

After the retreat, meditation became a part of my daily life. I would sit for half an hour every day and read about Buddha's teachings. I bought about a hundred audiotapes on dharma, done by Vipassanā teachers, and I would listen to them whenever I had extra time or when my emotions were off. I understood and agreed with much of what Buddha taught. I reminded myself that my life was not just about me, but that the biggest happiness came from helping others. This was a new beginning for me. Periodically, I still felt the need to go on meditation retreats so that I could remember how to find my center. I went to four meditation retreats in the next two years. I found it funny that I had never learned about Buddhism when I was in Japan, but stumbled upon these teachings in the United States.

In the summer of 2004, a friend of mine, Kazuyo, visited from Japan. She wanted me to drive her to San Diego. She wanted me to drive her to San Diego to see a psychic, Kathy, who was famous in Japan. Though I didn't have any particular interest in seeing a psychic, I figured that as long as I was there to take my friend and because I was always open to new experiences, I would have my first psychic reading. Kathy lived in a trailer in the mountains, in the suburbs of San Diego. The area gave me the impression that one might see UFOs there. It was in the middle of nowhere, and it seemed really close to the sky.

Kathy was a 50-something woman, blonde, big-boned, and weathered-looking, as if she had gone through a lot in her life and was somewhat run-down. The trailer, too, had a similar run-down quality. Kathy said she would channel a being called Lady Ashtar. I didn't expect much from the session, but I thought it would be an interesting experience, if nothing else. When it began, Kathy asked me to state my full name. Kathy told me that she was going to call in this entity who would answer my questions. Taking a deep breath, Kathy closed her eyes. It felt like an eternity of silence, but in reality it was about a minute later when she laughed in a husky voice unlike her own. For a few minutes, she told me about my past lives. Then she said she saw two roads in front of me. One went on and on without much change, but it continued to go downwards. The other road plunged down like a waterfall, but before it hit bottom, it moved up and up, and there was triumph at the end of it. She said I should take the second road. She then looked at me and said she could see some kind of box or container moving. It was a shipment from my furniture business. She also said I had two children—a son and a daughter. She told me that my son was shy and kind, similar to my personality; she also noted that he possessed a peaceful nature. Kathy added that my daughter was the opposite of my son, a bundle of energy but stubborn, and that she was a warm person who made everyone smile. Both descriptions were uncannily accurate.

How could you see that? I was thinking.

"You're thinking about a divorce, aren't you?" she asked. I was completely shocked. How could she have known that?

She described Tim as charismatic, overpowering, and controlling. She said he had issues with anger but could also be kind and generous. She told me that at times I felt that I couldn't breathe and was living as if I were walking on eggshells.

Then she asked the most surprising question: "Who is this old gentleman who says he is your father, although your real father is still alive?" I knew right away that it was my deceased uncle, who had considered himself a father to me. Kathy said he wanted to speak, and I told her to go ahead. He came into her, and started to talk just the way he ordinarily would, only in English rather than Japanese.

"I have seen everything," he said. "It is OK. You have tried everything. You can get a divorce."

"Normally," Kathy said, "older people like your uncle would tell you to stick with your marriage, so if he's saying you should get a divorce, he really means it." Tears were rolling down my cheeks. That was the last push I needed to get a divorce.

I should explain why this message from my uncle was so powerful. My aunt and uncle were like my second parents. In fact, I was "given" to them at birth as their child since my parents had four children and my aunt and uncle didn't have any. Growing up, I didn't know this; my parents were supposed to tell me when I became an adult. When I decided to move to United States, my aunt and uncle returned my birth certificate to my parents; it didn't make sense to tell me this because I wasn't coming back to Japan. My aunt and uncle were always very strict with me, but I knew deeply that they loved me, and they treated me as someone special. I only discovered this secret when I needed a birth certificate to apply for my green card after both my aunt and uncle passed away. I cried when I found this out because I regretted not having spent more time with them. I could have treated them more like my parents. Even though they were deceased, I always knew they were close to me.

So when my uncle spoke to me through Kathy, I knew what he wanted was what was best for me.

Chapter 3 Reflections

We live in a busy world. We forget to take the time to take care of ourselves. Many of us are taught that it is selfish to put our needs first, that our needs do not matter. The truth is that no one can love you the way you want to be loved. If you look for happiness, satisfaction, or approval from outside of yourself, you will always be disappointed. Because you are responsible for loving yourself, take care of yourself and make yourself happy. No one else can do that for you. It is your birthright to be happy and free. You have given your power to others all your life. It is time to reclaim that power and connect to the core of who you are.

What are the three things you have done in the past that you are proud of?

1. _____
_____
2. _____
_____
3. _____
_____

What are the three things you are grateful for?

1._____

_____

2._____

_____

3._____

_____

What are the three things you seek from others?

1._____

_____

2._____

_____

3._____

_____

Close your eyes, and take a deep breath. Open your eyes, and read the questions and the answers you have given. Take another deep breath, and tell yourself, "You are loved, you are loving, and you are lovable," three times. Take another deep breath, and close your eyes. Imagine giving and receiving what you seek from others. Like a mother taking care of a child, you can take care of your inner child; you do not need anyone else to do that for you. When you open your eyes, remember how you felt taking care of yourself.

CHAPTER 4

Taking Responsibility for Your Actions

The only person you are destined to become is the person you decide to be.
— Ralph Waldo Emerson

Coming from a traditional Japanese background, I knew that getting a divorce was not, in that culture, considered to be an honorable thing. It is proof that a person has failed, and it is to be avoided at any cost. Husbands and wives are supposed to take anything for the sake of their children, and it would be considered selfish to put them through such an ordeal. For years I told myself that I should wait until our children were older. Or that I should be happy because I could keep pampering myself and enjoying the luxury of doing only the things I wanted to do in life, and not rock the boat. But as I grew stronger and clearer through my spiritual work, and by being true to myself, I simply couldn't pretend any longer. My marriage was broken beyond repair, and my heart was so hurt that I needed major healing. In order to have restoration, I needed to be alone. If I stayed, another fight would just open my scars. It was a scary decision to make. I was living a comfortable life full of material success, with many helpers who made my life much easier. I was about to let go of most of this in order to be true to myself. And, even though my marriage wasn't working, it was something I was familiar with. Getting a divorce was like jumping into an ocean without knowing how deep the water was.

I was very sad that Tim and I hadn't been able to fix our relationship before it went so wrong. It wasn't just one person's fault. I wasn't the best person I could have been in the marriage. We both had done so much damage that there wasn't any way to reverse it, to turn back. For weeks, I cried. I knew separating would hurt my children, and that was the last thing in the world I wanted to do. It was the saddest decision I'd ever had to make in my life. But, though I wished I didn't have to, I knew what I needed to do. I also knew that my children would rather see me happy than see me stay in the marriage and keep hurting.

In July of 2005, I finally told Tim that I wanted a divorce, and that I was moving out. Tim didn't disagree, but he also didn't want to lose control of the business we'd started together. I took what I needed to live and left the company to him. Our friends told me that I was asking for a lot less than I deserved in the settlement, but I wanted to have a quick divorce, and didn't want to fight about anything. We agreed on joint custody of our children, with them spending equal time between Tim and me. I will never forget the day we told our children about our divorce. My son cried. My daughter was too young to really understand what was going on. She just smiled and said she could have two houses now. This is one of my most painful memories.

I moved out and rented a small house in the Pacific Palisades, the very first time I had ever lived by myself. I'd completely let go of my company, and so, for the first time since I was 21 years old, I wasn't a business owner either. Even though there were more concerns in my life, I also felt a different kind of peace and calmness that I had never felt before. This new house was mine, and it was a safe space for me.

The home was rustic and small, but one of the reasons I chose it was because of its warmth and peacefulness, and it was more than enough for me and my children. What I liked most about the house was that the backyard bordered a state park. The view was nothing but mountains, without any houses or lights to spoil it. I would even see deer and coyote there. I would often sit in the yard and meditate for a long time.

I usually began my meditation by "following my breath"—I took in a breath through my nose, let it flow to my heart, and returned the warm breath to the air through my neck and nose. I felt my feet and the bottom of my rear end touching the chair, establishing the connection to the Earth below. After a few minutes of this breathing process, I stopped following the breath, but my boundaries disappeared, and I became part of the whole, my being integrating with the nature around me and the entire Earth. In my mind, the words flowed as naturally as the breath through my body:

Where there is no self, there is no suffering. I am part of the whole nothingness, yet at the same time feel the everythingness. There is no need to change anything.

When I opened my eyes, I knew that whatever I was facing just is.

• • •

This was a good start for my new life.

Still, for the first year, I cried a lot when I was alone in my room at night. I cried because Tim and I couldn't make our marriage work—that we couldn't have done better. I cried because I couldn't see my children all the time, and, when they would call and say they missed me, I cried because I felt like I was a failure. I would often phone my mom and Akiko in Japan, and cry my eyes out to them. I don't know what I would have done without their support. But I never regretted my decision to get out of the marriage and start my life again. I was too young when I met Tim, and I was not the same person anymore. I had always relied on him because that was what he had wanted, and I'd never had my own life.

I was then 33 years old, and had the power to create a new life just the way I wanted it to be. I began dating Greg, who was also going through a divorce. His situation wasn't easy. Greg had three children of his own, and his divorce was more complicated than mine. Like me, he shared his business with his ex, but she wasn't going to leave the company, so they needed to find ways of working together after they'd separated. They fought over just about everything, from children, to business, to divorce settlements. But Greg and I stuck together as we went through the hardest time in our lives. I was grateful to have him in my life, as I wasn't strong enough to go through everything without his love and support.

For the next few years, I spent a lot of time meditating, practicing yoga, and traveling around the world. I didn't miss being tied to a business at all, as it had come with so much responsibility. For the first time as an adult, I had a carefree life. Whenever we didn't have our children with us, Greg and I would travel to exotic places like Egypt, Machu Picchu, Scandinavia, Panama, Argentina, and Spain. I enjoyed experiencing different cultures, eating local food, and seeing the beauty of the different parts of the world. I didn't realize I was making pilgrimages, but I can now see more clearly that all of those trips were preparation for my spiritual growth. On one level, traveling to these far-off places served as a source of renewal. Experiencing the beauty of distant lands and meeting people from different cultures always recharged my batteries. On another level, however, I drew a deeper strength from the land itself. Even in places I had never visited, I had the sense of having been there before. As impossible as it might sound, it was as if I had resided in all those places in previous lives, and, by returning to them, I drew on the knowledge that I had once possessed.

During this period of travel and meditation, Tim was angry with me, but he was going through his own period of adjustment. Once he remarried, we had an amicable relationship. I always appreciated that, whenever the children wanted to see me or spend an extra day with me, Tim would allow them to. Those first years were difficult, getting used to the routine of sending them back and forth, but they adapted beautifully and thrived in their new environment. My children gave me the hope and love I needed to transition into the next phase of my life.

I still remember putting my son to sleep one night about a year after our divorce. "Mom, I am OK now," he said to me. "You and Dad don't hate each other. I see my friend's parents fight all the time when I go to sleepovers. I see you and Daddy happy now, and I am glad." My son is an angel, and he had no idea how his words eased my guilty conscience that night.

I believe in taking action, no matter how difficult the road ahead is. If you don't face what's in front of you, either you are living a lie, or that thing will keep showing up in your life until you take care of it. The sooner you take care of it, the sooner you can move on to your next step. Most people are paralyzed by fear. But fear exists only in your thoughts. I believe that, if you are scared of fire and keep getting close to it without facing it, you'll continue getting burned and getting hurt. If you gather your courage and go through the fire, it will hurt while you are in the midst of it, but you will come out the other side and not have to face it again.

Chapter 4 Reflections

Many of us believe that we are powerless and cannot change the situation or struggle we are in. That is far from the truth, because you have all the power in the world to do anything you wish in the present moment. We keep telling ourselves that we do not have choice. But we do have choice, and no one can control you unless you give your power away. You are more powerful than you can ever imagine. You feel small and powerless because you don't believe in your power. It is time for you to realize that you are powerful enough to change anything in your life that you wish.

What are the three things you need to change about your life?

1._____

2._____

3._____

What would you feel if you could accomplish the changes you want to make?

1._____

_____

2._____

_____

3._____

_____

Can you find the creative solutions to bring the change in your life or take a small step toward the change?

1._____

_____

2._____

_____

3._____

_____

Close your eyes, and take a deep breath. Open your eyes, and read the questions and the answers you have given. Take another deep breath, and tell yourself, "I am in control of my life, and I can do anything I wish." Take another deep breath, and close your eyes. Imagine making the changes you want to make. When you open your eyes, remember the feeling of how it felt to accomplish them.

CHAPTER 5

Unfinished Business

Happiness is not something ready made. It comes from your own actions. – Dalai Lama

In the summer of 2009, I took my children to Japan for a vacation. Tim was traveling in an Indonesian jungle at the same time, and no one really had access to him. It was then that I received an email from the president of our furniture company. He said that he was quitting, effective that Friday afternoon. I hadn't been directly involved in the business since 2005, but I still knew that the company was going through a tough time. The economy had been very slow, and the business was transitioning from wholesale to retail. My monthly payments were sometimes delayed, and I had been told that cash flow was tight, but I hadn't expected this kind of urgent issue!

I tried contacting Tim, and even got in touch with his wife's brother, who was in the United States, trying to speak to him, or have him read the email I'd sent. I phoned the company's headquarters and asked the office manager if she could hold the business together for a week, until I got back from our vacation. Thankfully, she said that she could handle it.

Tim wasn't supposed to return for another two weeks, so, once I got back to Los Angeles, I went to the office to find out what had happened. No one had known the president was leaving, so everyone was in a state of shock.

After he came back from Indonesia, Tim begged me to take care of the business. He had the vision that the company needed, but he had always had someone else to do the actual work of managing its day-to-day running.

I hadn't expected to go back to running the furniture company. Maybe it was because I'd had enough rest—four years, to be exact—or because I had matured, but I could examine the situation with totally fresh eyes. I was getting bored with doing nothing and had been thinking about starting something new. So I figured that I would spend the next three months managing the business, tying up some loose ends. I could clearly see what needed to happen with the company, and the direction it had to take. This business was my baby, after all, and I was familiar with every thing and every job in it. After studying the business for a month, I told Tim that I could run it as its president, if he wanted me to. He jumped on my offer.

The first thing I did was ask my sister Akiko to come back to the business and take control of the container schedule. By that point, we had 15 locations in the United States, and were buying from five countries. With so many locations, and so many suppliers around the world, taking care of our inventory was the most important position in the company, and I knew no one was as capable as my sister of doing the job. I visited all our locations in my first year. Some of the older managers were glad to see me back, as I had the power to make decisions on things right away. I had no problem taking responsibility for those decisions, and I made sure my employees knew that they were welcome to call me if they ever needed anything.

In that first year, I also visited all our suppliers. I hadn't been to Indonesia in over 12 years, and our suppliers were happy to see that Akiko and I had come back, knowing that we would take good care of them. I set the company's priorities straight, and paying our suppliers on time was the first order of business. I knew that, if we paid them properly, they would be loyal to us and would work hard to keep our business. When Tim and I first began building the business 14 or 15 years before, most of our suppliers had been struggling, as they were just starting up and had almost no other customers or business. Now, however, most of them were the biggest suppliers in town, but they remembered how we took care of them at the beginning.

The company turned around immediately, and our sales improved right away. We were growing again. In the next four years, in fact, we experienced growth like no other furniture company in the United States at that time. We opened nine more locations, meaning that we had 24 successful stores.

For the first two years, I was working almost full-time. I moved into a bigger house, just a block from Tim's, in Brentwood Park. The house was a gift to myself. I was back in business mode, and in the beginning I loved every minute of it.

It was as if I hadn't quite finished what I'd started last time. After I had gained complete control of the company, I started to take more time off and let others run things.

Our company was solid and strong again. Unfortunately, I couldn't say the same of my relationship with Tim. We would fight and disagree over many business issues, and, when situations grew ugly, our personal problems would often come to the surface. Our relationship was not getting any healthier. I had divorced him many years ago, but by running our company I was reliving some of the worst parts of my old life all over again.

I was happy with what the company had accomplished, and where it was going since I'd taken it over, but at the same time I felt that I was ready to move on to the next chapter of my life. Coming back to run the company had been like taking in a child who was returning from college. I'd needed to take care of it for a short period of time, but now it was ready to stand on its own two feet. In fact, seeking closure with the business was essential to moving on. Literally and figuratively, unfinished business can be an obstacle to moving forward. After building the company up and leaving it in good hands, I was ready for the next challenge. From a more practical standpoint, my success with the business enabled me to become financially independent. My spiritual journey required an investment in psychics, healers, and others, and I was able to afford this investment because of our business success. This book, too, required money my additional work at the company provided.

Chapter 5 Reflections

We humans all have gifts to share with the world. Don't let your ego get in the way of finding your own special gift or talent. One gift or talent is not better than another—this is not a competition. You are very special, and your gifts can change those around you and beyond, no matter how small or how grand you think your gifts are. Have confidence in yourself, because you deserve it.

What are the three things you are good at?

1._____

_____

2._____

_____

3._____

_____

How do you feel when you are doing things you are good at?

1._____

_____

2._____

_____

3._____
_____

Can you find ways to share your gifts with others?

1._____
_____
2._____
_____
3._____
_____

Close your eyes, and take a deep breath. Open your eyes, and read the questions and the answers you have given. Take another deep breath, and tell yourself, "You are gifted and you can make a difference in this world by sharing your gifts." Take another deep breath, and close your eyes. Imagine yourself making the difference by sharing your gifts with others. When you open your eyes, remember how you felt while you were contributing to others.

I thought I was waking up. I could see that there were many women in the room, all working around me very busily. One to my left was sewing. It looked as though she was stitching beads onto material. Another woman was polishing jewelry—armbands and bracelets. Another was taking petals from flowers—I could smell them—and putting them into a vase. Then one of the women waved her hand, signaling for me to go to her. I walked over, and three women started draping a roll of cloth around me. As they rolled it around my body, they cut the fabric and took the pieces away. They were laboring quickly, in a hurry, as if there were a deadline they had to meet. Then I was led to another room, where there was a huge bathtub, almost like a small pool. I could smell lavender, rose, and eastern sandalwoods. I sank into the lukewarm water, and a woman began to wash my hair. She used three pitchers of different liquids, leaving one of them on for a long while. After the bath was over, three servants dried me, and I moved to the next room. They put the cloth they had measured earlier on me, and then they came in carrying a beautiful dress, which was white with gold woven throughout it. I was sat in a large chair, and women began to do my hair and makeup. They were making me so beautiful. I felt myself growing very excited and happy. I began to realize that I was preparing for my wedding.

PART II

Journey: Within and Beyond

CHAPTER 6

Spiritual Growth

*You can never cross the ocean until you
have the courage to lose sight of the shore.*
— Christopher Columbus

Ever since I had my first reading with Kathy, the psychic in San Diego, I was drawn to seek the help of those who could see or hear beyond our normal ability. I believed these individuals were sent to help me navigate this world, so why shouldn't I use their gifts? There is a story in Buddhism that goes as follows:

Once, there was a man who was very religious. When a terrible storm struck his town, everything was flooded, and he sat on his roof, waiting for God to save him. Then a rescue boat came along.

"Jump in," its skipper said.

"No thank you," said the man. "I'm waiting for God to save me." Then a helicopter came along.

"Take the rope," its pilot said.

"I'm waiting for God to save me," he replied. Eventually, the man drowned in the rising waters. When he was taken into Heaven, the man had his meeting with God.

"Why didn't you save me?" the man asked.

"I sent you a boat and a helicopter," God answered. "What else could I have done?"

While I valued the opinions of psychics, that didn't mean I had to see them every week, or that every decision had to be made by them. When I was going through a difficult period in my divorce, for example, I was seeing one psychic in Beverly Hills every three to four months. She would confirm what I already knew, but it was comforting to have someone assure me that there would be an end to my suffering. I found it fascinating that some people had the ability to help others with these unique skills.

After my divorce, I had a lot of time for myself, since my son and daughter were with Tim two weeks out of every month. While they were away, I would travel with Greg, or read books, or go on retreat. Periodically, I went to the Esalen Institute in Big Sur and took seminars there. The ground in Big Sur is sacred, and I could feel this when I was there. At Esalen, I would sit in the natural hot springs, which were on a high cliff above the ocean. My favorite time to soak in the springs was at night, when countless stars were out, and I could hear the ocean crashing against the cliff.

Sedona is another place I enjoyed. I loved to go on vortex hikes and meditate on the red rocks. At a yoga retreat at the Esalen Institute, I met a Japanese woman named Mako who lived in Sedona. Our children were close in age, so our families became good friends. My children also loved going to Sedona, and we would hike the red rocks together. On one of our first trips there, Mako introduced us to a woman who had the gift of healing families. This healer told me that my son was an old soul, and that in his present life he had come to Earth to take care of me. She said that we could even communicate with each other through telepathy. By that point, I already knew that my son was an "Indigo Child." From birth, he was able to see people's auras and spirits. I was glad that she could see this about my son, too. She also told me that my daughter and I were sisters in our past lives, and this made a lot of sense to me.

My heritage and essential nature helped me accept this and other ideas that might have raised skepticism in others. Japanese people possess an inherent open-mindedness and truly believe that certain people are in our lives for good reasons and that we are connected beyond this lifetime. I was also more open than most people and always was receptive to messages from the other world if my intuition told me they were true. Because I had felt a special connection with my son from his birth, I immediately understood his role as an old soul. As for the extraordinary concept that my daughter was my sister in a past life, I also found that to make perfect sense. We weren't just mother and daughter but had the relationship of siblings, and this perspective helped me understand our relationship better. I always felt that I was being watched over, so I was very appreciative of this healer as well as others who came into my life and helped me with my journey.

My developing spirituality was a natural progression. I

had been meditating and practicing yoga for years without knowing that was the beginning of my spiritual journey. I was being led to each stage of this journey; the Universe was sending me the right healers, psychics, books, and other tools so I could move forward. Nothing was out of my comfort zone, and I never had doubts or felt skeptical. From the very beginning, I could tell if someone was real or was faking. When I sensed they were real, I trusted them completely. As for vortices or places with energy, I felt them in my body—they too were true. It also helped that my sister, Akiko, was always very supportive about what I was experiencing. My mom wouldn't or couldn't understand my journey in its particulars, but both Akiko and my mom met a few of my healers and psychics, and they were blown away by what they could do or see. So this support, combined with my natural abilities and personality, allowed me to continue on my path.

During this time, I began to have an interest in many different subjects. I was introduced to astrology and numerology through some friends, and had my first astrology reading in 2006. My astrologer lived in San Francisco, so I had a phone reading.

"I'm going to explain who you are with more than 90 percent accuracy," she said during our first session. She went on to tell me who I was, what I liked, and what I didn't like. She knew my strengths and my weaknesses, and even my biggest fears! She could also read the charts of other people in my life, and was able to describe them as if she knew them very well. I was fascinated. How could she know so much just by the time and place of my birth? I then went on to read many books on the subject. Even today, I religiously read my monthly astrology forecast. Astrology is helpful because it can let you know what periods are most opportune for doing certain things—when the Universe and planets are sending extra help, or when the astronomical position is the opposite. Astrology would never control your life, and you always have the free will to do anything you want. However, in knowing the movements of the planets, you can avoid many headaches. Through being in harmony with the Universe, you can accomplish more. Studying astrology helped me tremendously, and I understood more clearly why certain things were happening in my own life. For example, I got divorced during the Saturn return.

I was opening up more, and learning about mysteries of life that I hadn't even known existed. At that point, I wasn't following Vipassanā meditation any longer but was learning from different teachers about different traditions. I was listening more to my intuition and keeping dream journals. I felt like I was a student again, but this time I actually wanted to learn. When I graduated from USC, I had vowed never to go back to school. I didn't like having been required to study subjects I didn't care for or wasn't interested in. I had felt that it was a waste of my time. But between 2002 and 2012, I must have read hundreds of books about personal development and spirituality. I was a sponge for knowledge, and I couldn't stop learning.

In the fall of 2010, I met a psychic named Kyle, who

would change my life forever. A Japanese girlfriend of mine in Malibu introduced us. She told me that I needed to see this psychic, because he was like no one else she had met. He could see auras, and could tell a person all about his or her life. I didn't have high hopes, but I felt as if there must be a reason his name and numbers were coming into my life at that particular time.

When I first met Kyle, he worked out of a run-down office in a small Studio City building complex. I almost never went to that side of town, and the place seemed shabby, especially in contrast to the office of the female psychic I'd been seeing in Beverly Hills for the last few years; her office was in a prestigious building right next to Rodeo Drive. Well-dressed and with many famous clients, she was someone who presented well.

I had spoken to Kyle earlier on the phone, and he had sounded nice and normal. But his voice had not prepared me for how physically large he was: Kyle could have passed for a lineman on a professional football team. He seemed especially big in his 500-square-foot office. I guessed he must be somewhere around 35 or 40, and he possessed a sweet, even cute, face. He directed me to a brown leather two-seater sofa close to the window and he sat across from me on a brown leather chair. There was a small coffee table between us, and he offered me water. Kyle was drinking a super-sized soft drink from a fast-food restaurant. The thought that popped into my head was, "He's like a big teddy bear turned into a human."

All my friends at that time worked out religiously and were healthy and fit. So I was taken aback by Kyle's soft drink and his size. But I chided myself for being judgmental, thinking, "Calm down. You need to stop thinking about his appearance. Besides, he's a psychic and can probably tell what you're thinking, so you're being extremely rude."

Kyle left the room for a moment, and when he returned he started our session. I knew right away that he was really gifted. He was confident yet kind, and he chose his words well. I could tell he had a sweet soul. He was very wise and yet charming and funny. He wanted the best for me, and he was willing to help me see the truth. I trusted him right away. While I had seen many psychics and healers before Kyle, he was clearly different. Not only was he tremendously gifted as a psychic, but he would become one of my closest friends and an indispensable guide on my journey.

Kyle began by telling me about himself, that his guardian angel had first come to him when he was 14 years old. Ever since, he has been able to see people's auras and other facets of their personalities and destinies. He also told me that we all have a guardian angel or two who stay with us through our entire lives. I had never heard or read anything like this from other psychics, so Kyle grabbed my attention right away; I wanted to speak to my angels.

Then Kyle started to stare at my head. His eyes darted back and forth as if he were counting. He then explained that he was reading my aura. He said that I have many layers of blue (I believe it was eight layers, and that was what he was counting) as my first color, four or five layers of tannish gold, and my third color was turquoise. Kyle explained that he calls it an aura, but what he actually sees is a person's life force or chi, so while aura changes depending on an individual's mood or time, a life force remains constant, since it represents one's personality. Kyle said that my many layers of blue meant I'm an old soul, and that I came to this Earth to leave a mark. My second color , tannish-gold, meant that I was a businesswoman, capable of accomplishing many tasks. My third layer, turquoise, meant that I was a caretaker—he could see I was a great mom and also liked to nurture people. Kyle could also identify spiraling purples, which meant that at some points in my life I was very spiritual, and at others less so.

Then Kyle went on to explain that I had a big heart and was a mother to everyone. He suggested that I would do well running a business, but I had no problem multitasking and being a super mom. He also correctly pointed out that I was well organized, that I made very few mistakes, and, if I did make a mistake, I wouldn't repeat it, given my perfectionist tendencies.

Kyle then told me that he could see people's relationships on their shoulders. He told me that all my family members and important friends were on my right shoulder while my partner and ex-partners were on my left shoulder. He detailed what he saw about my boyfriend Greg and also said that Tim was still on my left shoulder. Kyle explained Greg and Tim's personalities and their issues as if he were their best friend—I almost fell off the sofa. I love it when someone has such a gift and such clarity. I felt very comfortable with Kyle, and I knew deeply that I could trust him.

Then he went on to talk about what he saw on my right shoulder. He said that I was close to my mom, and that she was a powerful figure. My dad, he noted, wasn't as strong as my mom, and I wasn't very close to him. He saw my sister Akiko and said that I had very strong ties with her. At this point, I was very impressed with his skills and wanted to know more about how he could help me with my life.

• • •

I left his office with my next appointment booked in a few weeks' time, and, barely out the door, I was already eager to return. I told everyone I knew about Kyle, and Tim and Greg went to see him right away. During our next meeting, Kyle told me that I was here on this Earth to do something big. I wasn't sure if I believed him. He also told me that I had a guardian angel, and that I could meet him if I wanted to. Kyle explained that most people have one or two guides or teachers with them for a certain period of time. They come to a person to teach a lesson, and when a person masters this lesson, the guide will leave and go to someone else. Then a new teacher will come for the next lesson. But he said that, on top of my head, I had a doorway that led to a chamber of about 12 guides and teachers. Some were male, and some were female. Some were old, and some were young. They were all sitting at a table, and they would be with me for my entire life. Kyle said again that I must do some major work on this Earth. I was a bit overwhelmed with what he had told me, and I left the session somewhat in disbelief.

During the Christmas vacation, Mako came to L.A. with her children. By then I had known her for a couple of years, but she had never mentioned her healing work. This time, however, she wanted to give me healing sessions in return for my generosity toward her and her family. She told me that she did "multidimensional healings," where she would take a client's soul to different dimensions, conduct the healings there, and then bring the soul back into the body. I didn't understand what she was talking about, but I thought it would be an interesting experience, and I would never have declined an offer for healing.

After our children went to sleep, Mako began her healing session with me. "Close your eyes, and speak your name three times," she said.

I did as she requested, hearing my words float through the air, my name taking on a power as it was repeated.

Mako began to monitor my chakras and aura; she told me that she could know the state of a chakra by its color, size, and how fast it was rotating.

"Some of your chakras are weaker than others, but I can adjust them," Mako said.

"Do what you have to do."

She adjusted my energy. I felt a subtle shifting of forces within me, a rearrangement that didn't hurt but was profoundly moving.

"It is time to go to other dimensions," she said.

My eyes remained shut as warm energy flowed through

my body. It was an unfamilar sensation as I shifted into spheres beyond the Earth. It was as if I had been plugged into some celestial electrical socket, as if I were being connected to a power source that dwarfed anything man could create. As I flew skyward with Mako, I was suffused with warm, comforting energy. Something within me was changing.

Later, Mako explained that beings from these dimensions would keep sending their energy and working on my body throughout the night, even though I was coming back to my body.

Mako told me that she could speak to our higher selves, and she could converse with any beings or angels who might come down to talk to us during the session. There were some events in the future she could see, and she could answer certain questions if I wanted to know. I told Mako to just tell me what she saw.

"I see you traveling around the world and helping people," she said. "You are like Mother Teresa." She gave me a crystal called labradorite to keep—it was the first crystal I'd owned. When I held the labradorite, it sat cool in the palm of my hand, but at the same time I could feel it vibrating with a powerful, barely contained force.

After the session that night, I slept like a baby. The next day, I felt that my body and its energy were much lighter. When I spoke to Mako, I told her that Kyle had said similar things to me about my destiny to do something big in this world. At the time, I still didn't believe that I could do anything that would make this great difference they spoke of.

But I also felt it was such a coincidence having two psychics tell me something so similar to one another. When Mako and her family left for Sedona, she said that she could do long-distance healing sessions anywhere in the world, and, if I was interested, I could continue to work with her. So I agreed to monthly sessions.

As I noted earlier, I was astute about people—about knowing who was honest and who was not. I knew from the start that both Mako and Kyle were truth-tellers, and I knew it instinctively as well as cognitively. During Mako's sessions, I felt unique sensations that were authentic and powerful. Kyle couldn't have known so many things about me and about people around me had he not been able to see what others could not. Kyle and Mako knew deeply that, with the Universe's help, they were using their skills to make people's lives better. Their sincerity would be impossible to manufacture. I knew immediately and unequivocally that both of them had been sent to help me move forward with my journey.

My journey was getting interesting. I had never met anyone who could talk with, or see, angels, auras, or higher selves, and now two people in my life had proved to me that they could. Mako came back to Los Angeles the next month and gave healing sessions for my friends. I had another session with her, and what she did and said fascinated me. I couldn't actually see anything she was doing, but I definitely felt it. She told me that I was very special, and could go up into very high dimensions. Mako and I also went shopping for crystals together. I hadn't known anything about crystals, and it was astonishing to me that Mako could actually communicate with them. I told her that I wanted to do the same, and she gave me a book on the subject. She was one of my first teachers on "multidimensional healing," and I continued to work with her intensively for the next two years. I am very grateful for all the healing sessions she gave me and her support in my spiritual growth and awakening. Had I not met Mako, it would have taken me many more years to accomplish what I did in a short period of time.

The book Mako gave me was *The Crystal Ally Cards: The Crystal Path to Self Knowledge*, by Naisha Ahsian. Naisha created these cards—50 crystals and five elemental cards, all of which carry the vibration and its gift by creating images in the computer. In her book, she explains in detail the meaning of each crystal and what kind of message each carries along with how to use the Crystal Ally cards. I loved the book and went on to look up Naisha Ahsian on the Internet. I wanted to know more about crystals, and I was ecstatic when I found out that Naisha had a training program called "Becoming the Human Crystal." I read about the program and realized it was a big commitment. I would have to spend a minimum of one hour a day, five days a week, meditating, and would have to do homework every week for six months! And all the students taking the course had to join a conference call twice a month. My curiosity took over, and I signed up for it.

Before the class began, I had a phone reading with Julie, my crystal course teacher. She used Crystal Ally cards for her readings and would tell me which crystals constituted my being and what they meant. Julie was quite a psychic herself, and she would use the tarot cards for the details of a reading. We became good friends and continued to have annual sessions. Julie told me that I had many cards such as Azeztulite, Kyanite, and Phenacite that indicated I was receiving, and connected to, higher dimensions and beings. She said I would be a great student.

She picked cards for me that were mostly from the Storm element, and crystals such as Azeztulite, which represents "Alternative Realities." The image of the card is an ancient Mayan temple in the ocean; small ships are gathering to refuel on the energy that the temple supplies. The message of this card is that Azeztulite is calling you to let go of any and all densities in your life, and embrace the higher energies that are waiting to move through you. This is the card of the priesthood, in that it heralds a time of dedication to service in the Light. This is one of the strongest cards, and it meant I was receiving information from the Universe.

Kyanite represents "Inner Bridges," suggesting I was the connection between people, things, and even dimensions. Phenacite represents "Initiation." In this image, a human spirit approaches the Phenacite and is walking through a doorway—the entrance to higher realms.

During the next six months, I learned a great deal about crystals. Naisha's material was informative and well put together, and I was quite impressed by it. Though the theory behind crystals can be somewhat complex, here are the basics. Crystals are energy transmitters, and their crystalline structure allows them to absorb, focus, and then transmit subtle electromagnetic energy. Crystals have a pure energy that vibrates at a fixed, stable, and unchangeable frequency, so when you are out of balance, the crystals' vibrations can come into contact with your own vibration. When they connect, the pure vibrations of the healing crystal will interact with and change your vibration, bringing that imbalance closer to harmony.

By the end of the course, I could pick up a crystal and feel its energy. Julie told me in my second reading that I possessed a special ability and that I could communicate with any crystal or stone. I didn't fully understand what she meant at that time, but a few years later her words became a reality.

Kyle's work with me complemented what I was doing with Mako, Julie, and others. Kyle and I became good friends, not only because of his psychic abilities, but because he possessed a terrific sense of humor and was a natural storyteller. Kyle had many experiences to draw upon, many of them extraordinary. He had been doing readings for decades, and he had deep knowledge of things unseen by most people on this Earth and beyond. Through his work, Kyle knew everyone from spiritual leaders to business leaders to famous celebrities. He was also very open and would share his knowledge freely with me. There was a purity to him, as if he were an alien creature, unburdened by all the distracting emotions that cause human beings to lose focus.

Kyle gave me a meditation exercise that would help me to meet my guardian angel. He told me to ask my guardian angel his name, and "Julian" was given to me. For four weeks, I had to pray to see him, but finally I woke up one night and my guardian angel was standing beside me. He smiled and disappeared. He was quite handsome, with dark hair and skin like an Italian. That was the only time I ever saw him, but his presence was so clear I could never forget his face. Kyle's angel could communicate with Julian, so my angel was able to communicate with me through this channel. According to Kyle, his angel and other spirits would talk to him all day and all night. I later learned that this was how Kyle was able to know everything about his clients. Everyone has a guardian angel, and he or she stays with a person all the time; thus, he or she knows everything about a person and what's happening around him or her. I know it's difficult to be convinced, but I believed that the Universe was giving me a shortcut: Kyle was giving me information so that I would be able to do what I was sent to Earth for.

Kyle had many high-profile clients, from famous actors, singers, and writers to successful businessmen and women from all over the world. Kyle was the psychic who told Lee Carroll that he was going to channel an entity and write a book related to this experience. He also gave him the title of the book, *Kryon*. Lee Carroll is an American channeler, speaker, and author who has written 12 books on channelings, derived from an entity he calls Kryon.

I was learning to be more intuitive, and learning more about how the spiritual world worked and why we're here on Earth. I could remember dreams vividly. At certain times, I would even dream of what was going to happen in the future. For instance, I dreamed of a business event that became reality a few months later.

In my dream, I received an email from one of my managers in Atlanta. The manager who wrote to me was a middle-aged woman who had spent years working for me. She wrote a long letter saying how she really enjoyed the job but had decided to leave the company. I was kind of shocked in my dream, not having anticipated that she would depart. The following day, I told the story to Kyle as well as to people who worked for me. Kyle said that a dream sometimes represents certain people but not necessarily the same person. A few months later, I received a letter from a female manager in our Dallas office, informing us that she had decided to resign in order to work with her husband. The parallels between the dream and reality gave me a chill. At the same time, the experience told me that I should trust my intuition (dreams being an intuitive state).

At this time in my life, people were arriving, one after another, suggesting books to read and telling me which healers I should go to. I understood that everyone was being led to give me this information, so, when the third person in one month mentioned Mount Shasta, I knew I had to go there.

Chapter 6 Reflections

I once heard a saying that "human beings are spiritual beings having human experiences." I agree. But we all forget our connection to our soul because that is part of our agreement to come to Earth. At our soul level, we are nothing but one, loving and compassionate. I always remind myself and my body where I come from, following a few simple meditations that I will share with you. I have learned many different meditation techniques from many teachers and traditions, but the following meditation is the easiest. I will start with the simplest here, and I will add more complex meditations later. You might want to record the following meditation in your own voice first and play it while you meditate, as this is a guided meditation. Or you may choose to go to my website, www.astarchild.com, to listen to my recording of Guided Meditation 1.

Find a comfortable place where you won't be distracted for five minutes. I like to do my meditation sitting on a cushion with my spine straight, but you can find ways that are comfortable for you, perhaps sitting on a chair or lying down. Meditation is one of the methods to connect to your soul, and there is no right way or wrong way to do so. If this is your first time meditating, be gentle with yourself. You may not feel anything. Try not to seek the results, but instead just take the new energy into your breath and body. That is enough. Relax and enjoy!

Guided Meditation 1 by Ariyana ~a star child~

(You might want to set the alarm for five minutes or any length of time you wish to meditate.)

Close your eyes. Take a deep breath in and out. Take another deep breath in and out. Throughout the meditation, remember to breathe in and out consciously. Your breath is the key to staying in the present moment. Imagine yourself inside a white bubble that covers your entire body. You are breathing white light in and out of your nose. Inside this white bubble, you are protected from the outside world. It is a safe and comfortable space for you. Breathe the air in and out. Listen to your breath coming in and going out. Find the rhythm of your breath, and stay with it. When you are ready, open your eyes and come back to your body.

What did you experience?

1._____
_____
2._____
_____
3._____
_____

CHAPTER 7

Awakening

*There are many paths to enlightenment.
Be sure to take one with a heart.* – Lao Tzu

In July of 2011, I found a healer who gave guided spiritual tours of Mount Shasta. I decided to take my son with me and make it a mother/son trip. He was then 13 years old, and I thought he was ready for such a spiritual journey. I'd read that the entire area of Mount Shasta was a vortex that included a fifth-dimensional city named Telos, which was underneath the mountain itself. It has been said that, when Lemuria was submerged and destroyed, its inhabitants moved a few of its important temples and people beneath Mount Shasta. Many people believed this myth to be true, and I was ready to find out for myself. I always asked Kyle what I should expect from my trips. At this point in my life, every trip had meaning beyond the ordinary—there was also something to learn or an ability to gain. On this trip to Mount Shasta, Kyle looked into my future and told me that I was going to meet beings whom I would channel in the future. More excited than surprised, I anticipated that the trip might provide me with a breakthrough.

Here on Earth, we live in a third-dimensional existence. At the fifth-dimensional level, there is no physical embodiment. The island of Lemuria was said to be the sister island of Atlantis, and my reading and experiences taught me that beings from star planets such as Pleiades and Sirius came to Earth and used these islands to help humans. Lemuria was thought to have existed somewhere in the South Pacific, around New Zealand, and Atlantis was thought to be found somewhere in the Mediterranean Sea.

Mount Shasta is a sleepy little town, much smaller than Sedona. My son and I met the healer, Terry, at her downtown office. Terry first drove us to a lake. We sat by the edge of the water, and she told us to close our eyes and talk to our higher-selves. After five minutes of meditation, Terry asked us what our higher-selves had said. When my son readily relayed that his higher-self had told that him that he was pleased to see him at Mount Shasta and hoped he had a good day, I was astonished at his facility. It had taken me months before I could even get a feeling of what my higher-self was saying, and it had only taken my son five minutes. I was so happy for him. I then told Terry what I felt my higher-self had said—be open, learn, and enjoy new experiences—and she agreed that this was excellent advice for me. Once again, it seemed I was meeting with another healer who could see and speak with these higher beings. The three of us went to a few more sacred spots and vortices within the greater vortex of Mount Shasta in order to meditate. At one of these sacred spots, I actually saw my higher-self for the first time. This self was tall and angelic and dressed completely in white, and the experience of encountering this higher-self was mystical and fulfilling.

Terry was quite taken with my son. She pulled me aside and told me that his higher-self had told her not to interfere with him, as he was taking care of my son himself. She also said that my son could be a very powerful healer when he grew up, if he wanted to, and that he would be able to move objects through the power of his mind or intentions.

About halfway through our adventure, Terry asked me if she could check my aura. When she did, she was stunned to see that there was a huge scar on my back. She said that I carried so much love, and had such an open heart, she couldn't believe that I would carry something like that with me. She told me that it was from Tim, and that I was still bearing his spiritual attack. She worked on my aura, and healed the scar. All of this was after I had been working with Mako on a monthly basis, cutting ties with the people who had been taking my energy. In fact, it took another year of working with many different healers for Mako to finally say that my aura didn't need adjusting, that I was strong and centered enough to learn how to return to wholeness on my own.

On our last stop, we went deep into the mountain and stopped in a small clearing. Terry told us that the clearing was where we could be transported down into Telos in a transparent elevator. Terry explained that not everyone is able to take this journey but that we had received permission. She said that once we reached Telos, our family members would greet us and take us to their home. The three of us sat down and began meditating. As I visualized leaving my body and going down in the transparent elevator, I saw everything around me dissolving into ocean. For a few seconds, I seemed suspended in flight above the water. Then I arrived at what looked like the inside of a large spaceship. Before me stood several aliens who watched me closely. One of them came forward and spoke to me as if he was saying "welcome." They all had big, bold heads with large black eyes. I wasn't sure if I was dreaming, but as I was looking around the spaceship I heard Terry ask my son and me if we were done.

I was in disbelief at what had just happened. But when I opened my eyes, I had a strange feeling that anything is possible at Mount Shasta. As much as my experience was very out of this world, sharing it with Terry and my son made it real and acceptable. I somehow knew they would understand me and listen to my story without any judgement.

Terry asked us to share what we perceived. My son went first and related his experience. He said that he had gone down into Telos, and that, once he was there, a tall, blond person had taken him to his home. It was very interesting to me that my son had never heard of Telos or Lemuria, yet his description of the person he'd met was exactly like what I'd read about in books. After that, Terry looked at me, and asked how my trip had went. I told her that instead of going down into Telos, I went through the ocean, and to a spaceship. Terry closed her eyes, and said this was what she saw as well. She asked me what the aliens had said, and I told her that I hadn't been able to understand them. Then Terry asked me to close my eyes once more, and to go back to where I'd just come from, saying that she would come with me. I was hesitant, fearing that once again I would fail to understand what they were trying to communicate. But I overcame my anxiety and closed my eyes, and I was in the spaceship again. This time, I was told that these aliens were my family members, and that they were always with me. They explained that they were in my heart, and, as they did so, I felt it grow very warm. When I returned to Mount Shasta, tears were rolling down my cheeks, and I knew that what was being told to me was true. I felt the love they shared with me deeply. It was as if I had been yearning to meet them for a long time, and now that we had met we would be connected forever.

The trip to Mount Shasta was a very valuable one, and I felt that my son and I had grown closer through our shared experiences. When we were back in Los Angeles, my son learned from Kyle how to communicate with his guardian angel, and he has been continuing his spiritual growth ever since. Now he is 16 years old, and he is still speaking with his angel and seeing auras.

My son adapted quickly and naturally to the spiritual realm. He has been able since birth to see people's auras and spirits in his biological eyes (most people see them in the non biological "third eye"). He has also gone through his *recalibration*, (when his body is being reformatted, so that it can carry higher vibrations, and access more information) and possesses the ability to hear high-pitched tones, so my son's reality is very different than that of most people. He recognizes that not everyone can see what he can or understand what he knows. Wisely, he refrains from talking to people about his experiences unless they too have had similar experiences and possess similar capabilities. He talks to Kyle very openly because they can see the same things.

...

After the trip, I became very interested in channeling and was led to read many books on the subject. I learned about actual psychics and mediums, like Jane Robert's Seth, Lee Carroll's Kryon, and Edgar Cayce's prophetic abilities. I also read books on how to begin channeling. The material by Sanaya Roman was very educational and useful for a beginner. Kyle would often joke that I would one day channel a male being who would speak in a heavy British accent; he often speaks with the accent of an elderly British man to amuse me.

On August 5, 2011, Greg organized my 40th birthday party. About 50 people came, and, as a birthday gift, Kyle gave free readings to my guests. About a third of the guests, however, were Greg's yoga buddies. I had stopped going to yoga classes, as I preferred to do it by myself in my own home, so I didn't really feel connected to most of them. Another third of the guests were my employees and business associates, like my accountants and financial advisor. The rest were my family, close friends, and my spiritual inner circle. My sister Akiko was there with her children, and I had a great time with her. Greg didn't quite understand why I would devote so much time to spirituality. It was an urge I felt deep within me, and I knew I couldn't explain it to him even if I tried.

By the fall of 2011, I started seeing signs that my relationship with Greg was coming back full circle. When we took our final trip to Rome for Thanksgiving that year, I knew that it was time for me to move on. Through a few vivid dreams, I had seen that my relationship was over. We had helped each other when we'd needed it most, and we would always remember the good times we shared—I am still grateful that we almost never fought during our six years together. All my friends were stunned that I left the relationship so abruptly. Most people would have stayed because they didn't want to be alone, or at least until they had found someone else. But I couldn't stay if I knew in my heart that I was not getting anything from the relationship. And when I was done with people or things, I would let go completely. It was the first time in my adult life that I wasn't in a relationship. It was scary, but it felt right. I also realized how much energy I had been putting into our relationship, and I was depleted. I was led back to the Pacific Palisades, and the home that I live in now once again borders the state park. The land that my house sits on used to be considered a sacred space by the Chumash Indians. The home is beautiful, peaceful, spacious, and luxurious. I couldn't believe that I deserved to have it, but I later found out that the Universe wanted me to stay here and to do work from this place in the future. I felt that I was yet again turning the page to a new chapter in my life.

Not having a partner for the first time was a strange

feeling, even if the decision to leave Greg had been the right one. I was used to always being with someone. But I also found that I now had so much more energy for myself and for my children. The thing I perhaps found oddest was not having someone special to call at the end of the day, or in my bed, to discuss my life with. I was sad, but at the same time I felt free. I loved being in relationships and couldn't live without loving someone, so I knew I would have another partner one day. But I wouldn't go out with someone simply because I didn't want to face my own insecurities. I knew it was a lesson I had to go through. I would have to wait to meet the right person—someone who would have done enough work on himself emotionally, spiritually, and financially to be a suitable match. Otherwise, the relationship wouldn't work. I had no clue that I would have to wait a long time before I met my next partner, but again I had no regret moving forward.

Kyle and I continued to work together. It felt as if I were his student, learning more and more about life, spirituality, and the reality of things. We would sometimes use hypnotherapy to open up my potential, or do past-life regressions. Kyle had been on his spiritual path for 30 years, and he had a lot to share, but he kept saying that I could do everything he did, and in the end I would be his teacher. I didn't really believe this, and, to be frank, I didn't really care, either. I knew that Kyle had been sent into my life for a very good reason, and I didn't need to know what it was. In addition to Kyle, I also continued to work with healers and teachers in Los Angeles and in different cities.

In February of 2012, Kyle and I took a trip to Phoenix to see a healer named Lisa. Lisa called herself an "energy doctor." She was amazing at getting rid of one's old ties, which could come from one's ancestors, past lives, or society more generally. We are connected and tied with cords (spiritually speaking; these connections are invisible) to many people, past lives, traditions, ancestors, and social pressures. Most of these ties do us little good. Some people are sapping your energy or some cords are keeping you stuck at a job, in a place, or in a relationship. So it is always good to work on getting rid of those unnecessary ties. Sometimes it is not easy to do this by yourself, so hiring good healers who can do this for you is beneficial.

I worked with Lisa weekly at first, then twice a month, then monthly for about a year. It was a very transformational process, and I could feel a difference as soon as I finished a session with her. Lisa would ask me to make a list of things that I wanted to change in my life. Then she would go into each change item and identify who was connected to the change and preventing me from making it. Lisa would cut the cord for me, and I would breathe in and out and experience that severing of ties. She calls herself an "energy doctor" because she clears people's energy through this process. Once she has done her work, she facilitates dreams coming true for her clients because she has removed the barriers that prevented them from achieving their highest potential.

When we were in Phoenix, Kyle mentioned that he knew a tarot reader who had just moved to Scottsdale. I wasn't going to refuse a great reading, so I told Kyle to call her up. Ellen was available, and agreed to come to my hotel the next day. During our session, she saw everything Kyle and Mako had been seeing, but she said that I would be more like Princess Diana, in that wherever she went, she gave hope. She was quite sure that this was what I was going to do. I could see what she was saying with her tarot cards, and it was fascinating. Many healers could see my future and had said the same thing as Ellen, but I hadn't been able to see or hear it for myself. With Ellen and her cards before me, however, it was different. That evening, I took Kyle and Ellen to dinner. Ellen said that I was the most powerful person she had ever read for, and she had read for members of Europe's royal families and the top businessmen in the world. I didn't understand the full meaning of what Ellen had been telling me, but I was glad to have another guide in my life.

Since then, Ellen has become a part of my support team. I call her for both personal and business questions. She has proved to be quite accurate, with one of her strengths being able to know or predict the timing of things. Ellen has her trusted guides and angels she communicates with and she is very good with tarot cards. Around the time that Ellen took on a more significant role in my life, I also learned how to read tarot, and to use the pendulum. As people around me already knew, I liked to study and to master what I was learning. I became quite good with the tarot cards and the pendulum. The latter is a process by which you swing an object from a string or wire. By following the pendulum's path, you can receive yes or no answers depending on which way it swings for you. Using the pendulum helps develop your intuition, and, in turn, your psychic abilities become sharper. As I became more proficient with tarot cards and pendulums, healers began calling me to ask questions.

In May 2012, I was led to England to visit Stonehenge. By that point, I knew that the family I had met at Mount Shasta had something to do with star nations, and that Stonehenge and the pyramids in Egypt had been built by beings from other planets. If you're at all skeptical about these statements, think about whether people thousands of years ago possessed the technical ability to build complex structures like Stonehenge and the pyramids. If you look at it logically, it actually makes more sense to believe that humans received assistance from advanced civilizations than that they somehow built these structures themselves.

Psychics had often mentioned my past life in Egypt to me, as well as my connection to the sun god Ra, and to the pyramids. These psychics also said that my life there had been similar to the one I was now living—I had contributed to human beings' awakening. My healers and psychics had also explained that, even though I didn't fully understand what I was doing, wherever I went, I would be given the information I needed from the land and its people.

Stonehenge didn't leave a big impression upon me, but I knew I'd received what I needed by being there. It was on that trip that I met a Scottish businessman named Roy. Roy held a powerful position in high finance in London. He was by far the smartest and best-dressed person I had ever dated. And since I had never worked for a big corporation, the stories he told were very interesting to me. For the next six months, I flew to London each month to spend a week with him. When he was busy at work, I would travel to Paris or Prague alone, and on the weekends, he and I would visit places like Amsterdam and Hamburg. I thought that the British were more similar to the Japanese than Americans were, and I felt more at home in Europe than I did in the United States. Maybe I would move there after my children went off to college, I thought. But the long distance, Roy's hectic work schedule, and the ugly weather in London made it impossible for me to consider our relationship as a serious one. Still, it was a refreshing period in my life, and it was nice to be with someone.

I have always been a good multitasker, and that means that I was adept at balancing the spiritual journey I was on with my responsibilities as businesswoman and mother as well as my need for companionship. At first glance, it might seem that these different spheres of my life were unrelated, but with hindsight I came to learn that everything is related. For instance, I discovered that the spiritual forces in my life were not pleased with all my traveling and with my relationship with Roy; these aspects of my life were draining energy that could be better used to pursue a larger life purpose. Eventually, they would be responsible for ending my relationship with Roy and limiting my travels.

Before that happened, though, I took my daughter to

Greece in July for our first big mother/daughter adventure. Greece was one of the countries I had always wanted to visit, and I was thrilled when my daughter chose it out of anywhere in the world. I was enticed by the beaches. When we went to the island of Mykonos, and into the Mediterranean Sea, my whole body was vibrating with happiness. Then, in Santorini, I couldn't believe the beauty. The sunset was an overwhelming sensory experience, one that reminded me of the transcendence, that nature makes possible. Greece, unlike Stonehenge, left quite an impression.

That August, my son and I went to Japan while my daughter attended a summer camp in Maine. I celebrated my 41st birthday there with my family, and Akiko wanted to climb Mount Fuji. (If you are Japanese, you want to climb Mount Fuji at least once in your life.) Mount Fuji is considered to be a power spot, and I thought it would be an opportunity of a lifetime to summit it, especially with my son and my sister. I had no idea how hard it would be! A bus took us halfway up the mountain, and we began climbing around 1:30 p.m. Then, for the next five straight hours, we just went up and up. As we got higher, the path became narrower and steeper. I thought I would die. I hadn't prepared for the sort of difficulty I found myself in. Had I known how challenging it would be, I would have prepared, walking and hiking more before I went to Japan. Finally, we arrived at the mountain house, where we could nap for a few hours. In order to get to the top of Mount Fuji and see the sunrise, we would have to wake up at midnight, and then start walking all over again.

The mountain was dark, crowded, and freezing cold. Our legs were extremely tired, and I could hardly move. We eventually reached the summit around 4:30 a.m. There, we had our breakfast and waited for dawn. We were above the clouds, and the sunrise was so beautiful and mysterious, I didn't feel that I was on this Earth. I was very proud that my family and I had made it the entire way. I was also glad that I wouldn't have to make the trek ever again. In a strange way, my climbing up Mount Fuji reminded me of my descent through Mount Shasta. Both required faith and perseverance, and both were more than worth the difficult journey.

By late 2012, I started hearing strange, high-pitched noises throughout the day. Sometimes they came in my right ear, sometimes in my left, and occasionally both ears would ring. Sometimes the sounds would be quite high-pitched, and sometimes they would be lower. They could become very loud, but mostly they didn't, and I was getting used to having them in the background. Kyle could hear them when he was with me.

"How can you tolerate that?" he asked. But it wasn't as though I had a choice. Kyle tried to make sense of what was happening, and he said that it sounded as though six layers of information were coming in, and that the human brain couldn't translate it.

Around this time, Kyle was teaching me about the meanings of dreams and how to control them. He told me that when he dreamt, he could move freely inside the dream. He could freeze the dream in the middle, and look for objects that might give him information. For example, if Kyle found himself in someone's house, he could stop the dream and look for something like a newspaper in order to find out the day and year he was in—or a photograph, so he'd know whose home he was in. He could also make parts of his dreams larger, so that he would be able to see certain things in greater detail. Kyle could even return to a dream in the future. He said that I was able to do the same thing, but hadn't yet mastered the skills. At least by that point, I would know for sure that I was dreaming and that what I was experiencing wasn't real.

I continued to discover and work with new healers, teachers, and channelers. I was led to learn about different beings in the Universe, such as Pleiadians, Sirians, and Arcturians. I had never thought that we were alone, but also never assumed that these beings had anything to do with me. In April 2013, I attended a retreat in the Pacific Palisades with a channeler who had received information from Arcturians. The seminar itself wasn't interesting, but I met a healer, Carol, who was from Toronto and who could work on the crystalline body. Like other healers, she could see the structure of a body outside of its physical boundaries. According to her, people carried crystals in their bodies, and those crystals would often become damaged and would need healing in order to bring a person back to health. I had never heard anything like this, and found her philosophies and methods insightful and effective. I asked to have a session with her, and afterwards, she told me that my crystalline body was very complicated, and that I would need a few more sessions in order to regain my full potential. Following this, I saw Kyle.

"What the hell do you have on top of your head?" he asked me.

"I don't see anything," I said. "You're the psychic, so you tell me what it is." But he had never seen it before. He said that it looked like a star-shaped polygon, and that it was rotating, sending colorful light out of each point. Kyle felt that I was taking information in and sending it out to the stars.

During that retreat, someone mentioned DNA activation art. I looked online and found a website that sold these pieces. They looked rather beautiful and could apparently activate sleeping DNA. According to the information before me, human beings were supposed to have more than two strands of DNA, and all one had to do was look at these pieces of art in order to awaken the rest. Why not try it? I thought. I read that Heidi, who made the activation art, was led to channel the images. I ordered all 24 and immediately started to meditate with them. All her art was attractive, interestingly shaped, and very different from anything I had seen in the past, yet it was familiar.

Many healers and artists all over the world practice DNA activation arts and DNA activation healing techniques. Most of them have received messages, either from beings from other dimensions or through meditating. The foundational belief behind DNA activation is that we possess more than two strands of DNA, and our human evolution depends on our opening additional strands. The ultimate goal of DNA activation is a spiritual awakening, fostered by triggering the multidimensional DNA codex to awaken our highest potential.

Heidi could also channel beings from the Universe, and she would give a person his or her own symbol after a reading with them. I thought this would be fun, so I set up a 20-minute phone reading with Heidi the following week. After taking a few moments of silence, Heidi evoked the entities she channeled, whom she called "the keepers of the dream." About 10 seconds later, these entities spoke through Heidi with a computer-like voice. They told me that I was a teacher and I would write a book. They also saw me giving lectures in front of large crowds.

"By the way," she said, "what is that on top of your head that looks like a star polygon, sending light in and out?"

She could see it! I told her that I believed I was from the star system and was exchanging messages with them. Heidi agreed. She also mentioned that I would meet my future partner in 2014. She said that this man and I had shared a past life in Egypt, and when the work that was my life's purpose began, he would come. After a few days, I received my symbol. It looked like a triangle with three stars on each point. During one of my sessions with Mako more than a year before, she had told me that I had come straight from a star, and that when I hit the ground on Earth, I had made an impression. It was exactly what Heidi had drawn. Heidi told me that she had drawn hundreds of symbols in the past, but mine was the first with stars in it. I was getting confirmation from every psychic I spoke to. By that point, I had to believe I wasn't dreaming. I had met more than 10 psychics, all living in different cities, none of whom knew each other, and each one had told me the same thing again and again.

Later that month, a healer friend mentioned a website where I could hear "light language" and "activations." I was curious, and went to the site right away. According to this website, the healer could speak the language spoken among the beings of star nations. She called it light language. These beings asked her to record some of their messages as "activations," which would enable some people on Earth to remember their star lineage. The light language that was being spoken was beautiful, and I felt strangely familiar with it. The notes fluted out in mesmerizing, vibrating rhythms, a cross between speech, song, and something totally other. Then I opened an old activation recording, and the sound I heard was something out of this world—even disturbing. The voice was disconcertingly low and sounded angry, with a rapid-fire cadence. But I couldn't stop listening to it again and again. I called Kyle right away, and told him that he needed to hear it as well. He laughed, but when he heard it, his reaction was exactly the same as mine: goosebumps, our bodies tingling with energy. We knew from past experience that, when we both reacted this way, something was about to happen.

Chapter 7 Reflections

I used to be a perfectionist and was my own harshest critic for a long time. When I realized that being so harsh was not doing me any good, I softened up and forgave myself. That is when I realized that you must be kind to yourself first before you can give that gift to others. Many of us carry so much guilt and so many expectations that we can't see how we are treating ourselves and others. The good news is that you can change this behavior right now by making a commitment to alter your behaviors.

What are the three things you regret the most in your life?

1._____

_____

2._____

_____

3._____

_____

What are the three things people have done to you that cause you to still hold grudges?

1._____

_____

2._____

_____

3._____

_____

Close your eyes, and take a deep breath. Open your eyes and read your response to the first of your three life regrets. Take another deep breath, and say out loud, "I forgive myself for what I have done because I did the best I could at that time." Take another deep breath, and do the same for the second and the third answers. Take another deep breath, and read your responses to first of your three grudges question. Take another deep breath, and say out loud, "I forgive you for what you have done because you did the best you could at that time." Take another deep breath, and do the same for the second and third answers. Close your eyes, and breathe in and out. When you open your eyes, feel the energy in your body.

Write down three emotions you felt when you opened your eyes:

1._____

_____

2._____

_____

3._____

_____

CHAPTER 8

Language of Light

The mystery of life isn't a problem to solve, but a reality to experience. – Frank Herbert

Later that night, after speaking to Kyle about the light sounds, I was meditating deeply and holding one of my crystals. I was listening to the high-pitched tone in my ear, and I began to hum that pitch. Then my voice took over, translating this unique humming into what sounded like a spoken song, though the words were not in any language I knew. I was stunned. I knew someday I would channel, but I never imagined that it wouldn't be in English or Japanese. But this being just took my body over and continued to speak, though its speaking cadence was more like singing. The being was female, and her voice sounded like whales. I called Kyle.

"Kyle," I said. "I started to speak this weird language, and you have to hear this." I then hummed for about a minute.

"Wow, that sounds like my angel speaking," Kyle said. At that time, I knew it was some sort of light language I was channeling.

That night, the being didn't want to stop. She carried on talking and singing. I became exhausted and took a long bath.

When I came out, I started to speak a completely different language. This time, it was similar to the activation I had heard before online. This being, however, was definitely male. He was loud, fast, and even felt angry. For half an hour, he continued to talk, and I lost my voice. I recorded what the beings said, hoping Kyle would be able to understand. As soon as I closed my eyes in bed, I fell asleep.

I called that language I was speaking "light language" because the sound I was making carried messages and light. It was very different from human language. When Ellen first heard my recording, she said that she could see light transmitting from the noises. It was as though vibrational sounds were carrying different lights, and she could feel it more than she could hear it. It could be felt in one's entire body and aura, instead of just in one's ears.

Things were getting interesting. I had been waiting for a sign for a long time, but I never imagined that I would channel something like this. What was I going to say to people? In fact, I told only people who were very close to me about these experiences. My kids laughed and told me to stop speaking about such things. My sister was surprised initially, but she understood I was telling the truth; she knew me well enough to recognize that I would never make up something like this. Even certain friends and acquaintances were aware that I was on an intense spiritual journey, and, given this awareness, weren't overly surprised by my experiences. The psychics and healers I knew, of course, believed me implicitly.

I was an educated businesswoman, and a very rational

one, too. But the night before, I had been speaking different light languages, and I wasn't making it up. It would have been impossible to make up something so unique anyway. Kyle came over and listened to the tape, but at that point, he couldn't understand what the beings were saying. I tried to speak the language again, but they wouldn't come.

My head was spinning, and in a way I was happy that something—or someone—big had finally come through. But, at the same time, I had never liked what I didn't understand, and I certainly didn't like the fact that I had no clue what these beings were saying. I also didn't know how I could bring them back to speak again! I meditated and tried to understand what was going on.

Two weeks later, Kyle and I decided to try to bring them in. I meditated deeply, holding different crystals. Then came the high-pitched tone. Kyle was trying to ask me questions, and I was answering in the light language. Kyle didn't understand what I was saying, but his angel attempted to translate. We were both frustrated. Then my voice really took over, and began telling stories. Along with my vibrating voice, my hands started to move very fast. It was as though I was working on invisible strands. Kyle's angel said that I was working with the universal grid—the substance and framework from which the Earth and other planets emerged—and that I had the ability to heal anything I wished.

That same day, Kyle had a client, Alex, who was in the hospital. Alex had had heart surgery, but after the procedure, he was stricken with an infection and a high temperature that the doctors couldn't figure out how to lower. I had once met Alex briefly when he came to Kyle for a reading that was scheduled after mine. So Kyle said, "Let's send a healing to Alex." I sent him healing through my voice and also worked on the universal grid by moving my fingers with great speed, adjusting the grid for Alex. This was not a planned effort but rather one that flowed from intention—once I set the intention and brought the tones that were needed to certain people or things and let my hands move, the healing took effect. Three hours later, Kyle called. He said that he'd just heard from Alex; the doctors didn't understand why, but his fever had broken. I smiled.

I was gratified and energized by this ability to heal; it was somehow related to my larger purpose, but for the moment my focus was on angels. Soon, Kyle's angel could translate most of what I was saying. Some things, however, his angel didn't have an English equivalent for and couldn't explain. The female entity was named Kyrah. She was pure, and she had the ability to clear people's karma, program crystals, and communicate with, or alter, almost any mineral on Earth. So when I held any crystal, I could vibrate with its energy. The male entity was named Prishnah. He claimed he had ultimate knowledge, and that he liked to be called "Professor Prishnah." He said that they came from the seventh dimension, that he was my father, and that Kyrah was my twin sister.

I was shocked at first to discover these truths, but ultimately it all made sense. I was told by Prishnah that he was my family member in Mount Shasta when I had visited there. So I had anticipated that he had a familial relationship with me. In addition, I had read many books by people channeling beings from other dimensions, and I somehow knew that things like this could be possible. I was excited to see what I could do with this information, since I had been told by many healers and psychics that I was going to play a role in the salvation of the Earth. Knowing that I was related to these powerful entities, then, was a relief; it told me that I possessed the power to accomplish what I would set out to do.

While my rational mind was struggling with this concept—that I was channeling beings beyond this Earth—Kyle confirmed that when Kyrah and Prishnah came, my aura changed from its original color. He explained that the particular color of an aura was a litmus test; it was how he could tell if someone was really channeling or just faking. When another entity enters that of a human, the latter's aura changes from its original color into the color of the entity's. As mentioned before, my usual aura was blue, tannish-gold, and turquoise. When Kyrah would come and speak, my aura color would turn completely purple. When Prishnah came, it would become dark blue. I knew instinctively that my son could understand the light languages I was speaking, and Prishnah confirmed that my son could certainly understand him and Kyrah if he wanted to.

I spoke to my crystal teacher, Julie, and she said that I should start programming crystals, so I ordered over a hundred pieces of clear quartz. I sat and programmed them for the next week or two. I had learned to make crystal grids during the crystal course I had taken, and I already had them in some of the rooms of my house. Crystals have the ability to communicate with each other, and by placing them geometrically according to a stone's structure, the energy inside the grid becomes amplified and very powerful. In my meditation room, I had a grid with six clear quartz crystals using five elemental crystals, as well as one programmed with my higher-self energy. After I had programmed about 36 pieces of the quartz, I made a second grid around my meditation seats, and I would sit and meditate there often. When I showed Kyle this room, he said, "It looks like you're floating in some other dimensions in there." The energy was so strong that he couldn't even come inside without feeling dizzy.

By then, I was learning to summon Kyrah and Prishnah simply through my will. I would hold a crystal, and Kyrah would hum again. It was while I was experiencing different crystals with Kyrah that I had vivid flashbacks of my past life. In one, I was male, and holding crystals. It was the time of Atlantis, and I knew the city was going to be submerged. I was the record keeper of that civilization, and I intended to come back to Earth so that I could unlock the messages I had left for myself in the future.

The flashback was so lucid and shocking, that it came with all the conviction of reality. I called Kyle and told him about it. Kyle said he had already seen this past life of mine, and that his angel had told him I was the record keeper for Atlantis. Later on, a few other psychics confirmed this as well.

As I saw it, the important question wasn't whether I was the record keeper, but rather, if I had these abilities, how could I use them to help Earth and humanity? I had no doubt in my mind that I was brought here to be of service, and that I had been preparing for it for many years—possibly many lifetimes.

In May, I went to visit a healer, Carol, in Toronto. While I was there, a friend of hers heard about me and asked if I would program a crystal for her. She wanted to put it under the river in order to purify the water. So I set the intentions and programmed it; I held it in my right hand for a few minutes, directing energy into the crystal. Two weeks later, Carol called me and said that her friend was meditating with the crystal, and that she had started to speak some kind of light language! Because of this, her friend had kept the crystal, rather than putting it in the river. I remembered that Julie had mentioned something about this. She said that there were people all over the world who would be able to "download" what I programmed into the crystals, but these people were rare and had to have a high enough frequency in order to do so. When a person works on his or her spirituality or consciousness, one's frequency of energy vibrates higher and faster. If one is totally unconscious, one's energy is heavy and their frequency is low and slow. I was told by several different healers that they have never seen anyone who vibrates as fast as I do and that my frequency is beyond normal human capacity.

I spoke to Kyle about this issue, and he said that there

weren't many people who came from star systems, or who had past lives or future connections to planets other than Earth. I was the rare exception. This meant that people would not necessarily begin to speak light languages by meditating with crystals I had programmed, but I could program crystals so that people could awaken their highest potential. Maybe I could even heal people with crystals. So I started to program and give away crystals to the important people in my life.

Around the same time, I was becoming quite ill. My nose would run, and my eyes were itchy and red. It was as though I were experiencing an allergic reaction all day long. This was uncharacteristic for me. I had always been very healthy, and had never experienced issues with such an illness before. I hardly caught colds! When one of my employees from Miami came to stay with me and witnessed me blowing my nose, he said that in over 10 years, he had never seen me sick.

Kyle and I tried to understand what was going on. One of the explanations Kyrah and Prishnah gave us was that their temperature was colder than mine, and I was having a hard time adjusting to this. Another reason was that at night I was doing work in the Universe, where the pressure was very different than it was on Earth. Coming and going between the two was taking its toll on my body. They said, however, that the illness would go away. I would often cry because I was feeling so miserable between my allergy symptoms and not having enough sleep. My body ached as if I were 80 years old. I didn't think I could go on like that much longer.

Ellen felt that human beings weren't meant to carry so

much light, and that my cells needed to be recalibrated in order to receive and transmit more of it. The information seemed not only to be coming into me from the above, but also to be leaving my body and moving toward the Universe. It wasn't a one-way road. I wasn't only helping Earth—I was also sending the Universe the information it needed from Earth. We knew that this was just the beginning of where I was going.

In June, I asked Carol, Ellen, and Kyle to come to my house. I trusted them as my advisors, and each of them could communicate with other dimensions in their own ways. I wanted to bring Prishnah and Kyrah to them so together we could figure out my next step. By that point, Kyle could easily understand what Kyrah and Prishnah were saying. When all three sat down in my living room, I started to bring in Prishnah and Kyrah. To my surprise, Carol was struggling to accept what was taking place. While Carol possessed a cognitive understanding of all things spiritual, the reality of seeing angels was a challenge. Carol became quiet once I started speaking, and it seemed she didn't quite understand what was said or didn't want to get involved. I was a little disappointed with Carol's reaction, but Ellen reacted even better than I had expected. While she is usually more logical than emotional, Ellen believed completely in what I was trying to accomplish. She started to write down what Prishnah was saying in English. Ellen and Kyle discussed in detail what they could do and what questions to ask. At the beginning, my friends were looking to me for answers, but I didn't know why Prishnah and Kyrah were here or why I was able to speak their language. But they quickly recognized that I was functioning as a medium, and they accepted that that was my role. So Kyle and Ellen asked directly of Kyrah and Prishnah, "Why are you here, and what do you want to do?"

They said they were members of a Galactic Federation, and that I had volunteered to come to Earth at this time so that I could help humanity by bringing necessary information down from the Universe. Those in the Galactic Federation possessed much higher technologies or faculties and were using me to share their knowledge with humans.

All of us were thrilled with this response. Wouldn't it be amazing if I could communicate information for the betterment of humanity and Earth? I didn't doubt that these beings could do as they had suggested. I felt it deeply in my heart.

While Ellen and Kyle went outside to take a break, Kyrah and Prishnah kept talking. It seemed to me that they were quite happy that they could finally talk and someone could understand them. Then suddenly I started to speak in a completely different light language. It was similar to the one I had heard coming from the channeler online, yet it had its own unique aspects. Prishnah told me earlier that where they were from, the language I had heard online was a common universal language. It was similar to the way English is used on Earth. This new voice was definitely female, and she sounded like she was whispering something.

I called Kyle and Ellen back inside the house and asked them to listen to the new light language I started to speak.

Prishnah explained that her name was Novysha and that I shared my soul with her. Basically Novysha is my future self, and, in the place she came from, Novysha was considered to be a soul doctor. Novysha spoke for a long time until I lost my voice.

At this point, I was wondering if I would speak to many more entities other than my family. When asked, they said that I would speak to the three of them most of the time, but on occasion I would speak with time travelers.

Then something totally inexplicable happened. The living-room door swung open on its own. An eight-foot-tall man walked in; I couldn't see him, but Kyle and Ellen could. The tall man claimed he was a time traveler and that he was going to assist us. He spoke perfect English to Ellen and Kyle, so they could communicate with him. I had received another guide.

Before they left, Novysha said the man's name was Jerrest and that, like Prishnah, he possessed universal knowledge. From this point on, Jerrest was around me all the time like a guardian angel. After hours of hearing the angels speak and translating their words, I was drained, as were Kyle, Ellen, and Carol. The emotional exhaustion almost equalled the physical weariness, and none of us could continue. I thanked Kyle, Ellen, and Carol for their hard work that day, and then I collapsed into my bed. Though the angels were no longer speaking, they remained within me, ready to reemerge when needed.

Around that time, I started to give healing sessions. I

didn't charge because I was just trying to figure out my abilities. When I tried to offer healing, all three entities would merge, speaking at the same time, while I moved my hands. Normally, it would take me only 30 seconds to heal a person. Kyrah, Prishnah, and Novysha told me that these 30 seconds were the equivalent of two hours of hands-on healing by someone else on the Earth. They also said it was easier to heal minerals and Earth than it was to heal humans. I could heal human beings, but the problem was that they had free will, and there were many obstructions to their receiving my healing in a pure way.

My abilities allowed me to send healing to someone with headaches, easing the pain immediately. I did this for both Kyle and my son. I programmed a crystal and gave it to a breast cancer patient in Switzerland. As part of her treatment regimen, she was supposed to come back next year for another surgery in Los Angeles, but after putting my crystal on her breast, she didn't have to go through any more surgery. My healing doesn't always work since some people don't want to get better, and some are so enmeshed in emotional trauma (anger, jealousy, and so on) that it prevents the healing from working

For another three months, I continued to be sick, and my body continued to ache. I was miserable. I felt sorry for my children as well. They didn't understand why I didn't have any energy, or why I was unwell all the time. Kyle continued to talk to Kyrah, Prishnah, and Novysha, as well as to my new guide, Jerrest, so that we could gain more clarity as to what I was supposed to be doing on Earth. They explained that I was hearing high-pitched tones because I was recalibrating all the necessary information, not just from this Earth, but from other dimensions, too. Once the information was downloaded and recalibrated, I could use it whenever I needed it. They also told me that I was almost done with this process.

Kyle confirmed with Jerrest and the other three that I was working every night when I went to sleep. As soon as I closed my eyes, I would slip out of my body and go through a portal that was on the ceiling of my bedroom, right above my head. They said that I was collecting keys, which were necessary to my work. They also said that the crystals I had programmed in May were maps, and that I knew exactly where they led and where they belonged.

I started to withdraw from the world. I'd always felt I didn't quite fit in here, and the feeling was getting stronger. I didn't enjoy seeing people, and I certainly didn't enjoy being in large crowds. I felt that it took too much energy to be with others. I stopped reading books, and I stopped watching television or listening to the news. I even stopped meditating. I spent many hours at Korean spas getting massages, and while I was at home, I basically spent my days just taking care of my body so that I could function. I felt completely alone. I didn't want to eat any fancy meals. I didn't want to travel anywhere exotic. The things that had excited me in the past no longer had any hold over me. I had lost interest in being on this Earth. During my sessions with Kyle and Ellen, I would often cry or get angry. They both kept telling me that what I was going through would pass, and that they could clearly see a future for me in which I was happy and working. If it hadn't been for their conviction and support, I don't think I could have continued on with my life.

At this point, I only had my children half the time, so they didn't know exactly how sick I was. Like many moms, I hid my illness from them as best I could, not wanting to trouble them. I didn't have much energy, but I could manage the basics of taking care of my children. Despite my running nose, headache, and aching body, my illness was more internal than external.

I believed what Kyle and Ellen were telling me—that this illness would pass. So seeing a doctor seemed ridiculous. I couldn't imagine trying to explain to a science-focused person that I was sick because of doing the universal work and upgrading and recalibrating my physical body. Nonetheless, I was miserable and angry because of my condition. I was depressed and didn't want to continue to live. I also felt that people made this Earth a disaster by their greed and indifference, and I couldn't see why I had to save them from their character flaws. I was hating people at this time of my life, acting more like a patient than a savior.

In September, I gradually became better. The running nose and body aches ceased, and though I still got occasional headaches, the malaise lifted. Still, the three entities continued to tell Kyle that I was doing my important work at night. When I would complain, asking why I had to suffer so much, they would only say that I had signed a contract, and had volunteered to come here. What could I say to that? In fact, Kyrah, Prishnah, Novysha, and Jerrest were quite the comedians and would often tell jokes, making me laugh all the time. A part of me wished that I understood what they were saying, but another knew that this was for the best. If I had to translate what they were saying, it would force me to think twice about what was coming out of my mouth. If I was simply channeling the light languages, then I could just do it with confidence. I had Kyle, who could translate, and the three kept telling me that there would be others who would also be able to interpret the languages when my work went out to the public. I felt relieved to know that, if no one else was available, my son could always translate. They said everything was right on schedule.

That was a busy September. My 14-year-old daughter declared that she would be living just with me and not her father. For the first time in almost 10 years, I was a full-time mother again. The adjustment wasn't easy; I'd had so much freedom, for so long, that I'd been spoiled. And though my illness had abated, I was still regaining my strength and wasn't yet 100 percent. But having her full-time was very sweet. I had always felt bad that I'd gotten divorced when she was so young and that she'd suffered and missed me terribly for many years. This was now our time together to make up for what she had missed when she was young. My daughter was also in her final year of middle school at the school she had attended since preschool. My son had gone to another prestigious private school in Brentwood two years before, when he began ninth grade, but my daughter said that next fall, when she began high school, she would rather go to boarding school in Ojai, a town north of Los Angeles. For the next two months, I was very busy filling out applications and attending interviews.

As I noted earlier, I was an excellent multitasker. I was able to continue my daily routines and attend to my children's needs. My children always came first. In fact, I was also running the business as the president of the furniture company at this time, so I was managing all three (spiritual journey, work, and family) well.

In late September, Kyle told me that Prishnah had said I was going to have a visitor. During our next meeting, Kyle and I both meditated, and, sure enough, this strange sound began to come out of my mouth. I told Kyle that the visitor had come. His voice was similar to Kyrah's, but much deeper, and definitely male. He said that he was a time traveler. He had two bodies—one in the past and one in the future. He told us that when the past was changed, the future, at the same time, needed to be adjusted accordingly. And when the future was changed, the past needed to be adjusted. That's why he had two bodies, and lived in both places. His name was Laneesh, and he had come to work with me. Kyle drew a picture of him; he looked like a monkey in a space suit.

Chapter 8 Reflections

Life is a mystery. It comes with ups and downs. You think something is concrete, like love or money, and the next thing you know, you can lose it in a blink of an eye. Many people are lost in the past or live in the future and miss the present moment. You cannot live in the past or future, so let them go. Do not dwell on the past or future, as they are not here. Change is inevitable, so don't fight it, but instead learn to surf life's ever-changing waves.

What are the three things you faced in your life that were total surprises?

1._____

2._____

3._____

How have those experiences changed or shaped your life?

1._____

2._____

3._____

What have you learned from those experiences?

1._____

2._____

3._____

Close your eyes, and take a deep breath. Open your eyes, and read the questions and the answers you have given. Take another deep breath, and tell yourself, "Life is a mystery, and I am willing to face it." Take another deep breath, and close your eyes. Imagine that you are in front of a big white sheet of paper. You can pick up a crayon of any color and draw a door. Imagine yourself turning the handle, and walk through the door as if you are starting your new life at this moment. When you open your eyes, remember how you felt when you were walking through the door.

CHAPTER 9

Waiting for the Green Light

It does not matter how slowly you go as long as you do not stop. – Confucius

Things were changing. The arrival of Laneesh and my recovery from illness signaled that I was entering a new phase of my life. But I anticipated more changes ahead, and when my daughter moved in with me, one external change was followed by an internal one.

About a month after my daughter began living with me full-time, we both felt that we should get a puppy. I liked the silence, so I didn't mind when it was just the two of us, but the house was way too large for my daughter to be alone in when my son was with his father. My daughter picked a Japanese Chin, and we found a breeder in Washington State who had a four-week-old male. We fell in love with his picture, and waited until he was eight weeks old to pick him up. In Japan, though I had grown up with cats and a dog, I had never been a big fan of animals. But when this puppy came into my life, a different part of my heart opened up that I hadn't known existed. We named him Ren. He was the cutest, sweetest thing in the world, and having him was like having another child. A few weeks after Ren arrived, I was in the backyard, where he was running around. Our neighbor's cat, which I had seen several times in the past, just walked up to me and started to push her body against me. I couldn't believe my eyes. I patted her, but she didn't want to go away. Maybe, I thought, she had felt that my heart and love for animals had opened up.

Around the same time, Kyle did a reading in the city of Laguna Hills, and while there he was bitten by a spider. He woke up at his client's house the next morning, and had eight little spots on his wrist. I saw him the following day, and his wrist was red and inflamed—double its normal size. He asked if I would give him a healing because his angel told him that I could. I did, of course, and afterwards, he said he felt better, but I didn't hear from him over the weekend. When I did speak to him again, Kyle told me that the situation was getting worse, and he had to see a doctor. They took blood samples, but he was in a lot of pain, so for the next few days, I continued to send long-distance healing to him. After several days, he went back to see a doctor. He had some black spots on his wrist, and it was still red, but the swelling was almost entirely gone. His blood-test results were back: he had been bitten by a black widow spider!

His doctor couldn't believe his eyes. "What kind of lotion did you use?" he asked. "Your scar is healing, which usually takes three months after you've been bitten. And normally your entire wrist would have gone completely black. This is incredible!" Kyle just told him that his friend had been sending him healing. The doctor didn't believe him and kept shaking his head.

I continued my spiritual work at night while I was sleeping and ran the furniture company during the day. With the furniture business, I was working less than an hour a day, making sure everyone was doing his or her job. It wasn't until November, though, that I learned what my nightly spiritual work involved. Laneesh and Jerrest had been telling me that I was doing a very important job at night without specifying what that job was. I would wake up exhausted many mornings, so I recognized that I had been engaged in a challenging task, but I didn't remember what it was. As I noted earlier, I was irritated and frustrated by this lack of understanding and feeling of exhaustion upon waking. Even thought I knew I was contributing in some way, I had no evidence of what my contribution was. Finally, Jerrest explained to me (through Kyle) that I had opened a gateway from Earth to a new galaxy. From what I understood, without this new gateway, the faraway galaxy would have been doomed. This was one of the biggest jobs I had come to Earth to accomplish. I was proud upon learning that I had completed this mission and also felt relieved; if I had done nothing else in my human life, at least I did something major for the Universe. Jerrest told me that a temple had been built in honor of my work on the other side.

• • •

I had started creating the gateway in May when I first programmed a crystal, opening the doorway to that galaxy. It was a task that could be carried out only by a human on Earth. As part of this process, I programmed 36 crystals, each one representing a particular location, so when 36 crystals were placed in certain way, they made the map that was needed to open the doorway. I was told by the three that I knew exactly where each one belonged (even though my human consciousness wasn't aware of this). For months, I was told that I was collecting "keys" for the work, and I assumed that, after the crystal opened the doorway, I was collecting "keys" to open certain portals or specific areas of the doorway, and, after a few months of work, the entire portal would open to the other side.

Before being informed of the purpose of my nightly tasks, I had been complaining a lot, asking why I wasn't allowed to see what I was doing. The answer was always the same: to protect me from seeing the ugliness or harshness of what I was doing. I was told again and again that my work at night involved helping the Earth to correct its course or assist humans in disaster. Even the three said it was hard for them to see what was taking place, and they doubted that a human could handle this vision.

In any case, I finally became aware of what had been going on at night, and it was at that point that I removed the second grid from my meditation room because, as Kyle put it, the crystals were eating me alive by drawing on my energy. And, for the first time in months, I had my energy back.

I had been waiting to meet my life partner for over a year. In reality, I think I had been waiting for him through many lifetimes. This was quite frustrating, to say the least. After all, when I wanted something, I always went and got it. But Kyle and others agreed that timing is the hardest part, especially with a partner you haven't met, because it is not about just your journey, but his as well. I had seen him in my dreams several times by then, and all the psychics I had met (more than 15 at that point) were saying the same thing. We'd had happy past lives together in Egypt and were supposed to work together now on Earth. Everyone described him in the same way: he was handsome, powerful, and dark-haired. Some of the psychics even said that I could not begin my work until he showed up. The three and Jerrest said he was close and that I didn't have to worry. We were meant to meet. I was impatient, however, and felt that I had waited enough. But sometimes we don't have control, and I was sure that there was a reason for everything.

I finished all the applications for my daughter's schools in December, and I took my children to Japan for Christmas and the New Year. It was always a fun time to visit Japan, as New Year's is the biggest celebration there. It was also nice to see my parents and my family. I usually stayed at Akiko's house when I visited. She had bought land where my great-grandmother, my grandmother, and my uncle and aunt used to live and had built her house there. It seemed to me that every time I went back, there was some spiritual reason for it—perhaps it was finding closure with my ancestors or connecting back to this source.

After I got back from Japan, my ears would often still ring, and I started to have slight headaches. They would last for a few days, and then I would be back to normal. About a week after I'd returned to Los Angeles, Kyle became very sick. He had a horrible headache and couldn't get out of bed for days. His angel and the three told him that they were upgrading and recalibrating his system so that he could do further work with me. It was horrible to see what Kyle went through for the next two months. In order to upgrade and recalibrate his system, they worked on his brain, eyes, third eye, and everything else one could think of. The good news for me, however, was that I had already gone through the process the previous year, but since I wasn't clairvoyant, I couldn't see what they were doing to me. And like most women, I had a higher tolerance for pain than men. Kyle, on the other hand, could see everything that was happening to him, and he had to cope with watching these beings stick needles into his eyeballs and all other sorts of things. Then I got a call from Ellen, who said that she was having the same headaches. The three told Kyle that they were upgrading Ellen as well. Both Kyle and Ellen said that what they experienced was like being abducted by aliens in order to be worked on! But, after a few months, both had survived the upgrade.

When I first went through the recalibration process, I had complained to Kyle and Ellen about my physical discomfort, and they had reassured me that I would be fine, not recognizing the toll it took on me. When Kyle and Ellen went through it, they spent days in bed, barely able to move. Even though they, like me, would recover, it was a grueling process. But it was also a necessary one. We all needed to reach a high vibration and frequency level to do the work. My role was to receive and send information at the highest level, and their role was to translate what was received and work with me.

The three had told me in the past that I was clairsentient—that I know things instead of seeing or hearing them. When Kyle would hypnotize me and ask me all sorts of scientific questions, I would know the answers to questions that I had no rational way of knowing. I wouldn't see things like a film playing before me, as many clairvoyants like Kyle would, or hear like a clairaudient such as Ellen. I would simply know. It was hard to explain, but I had always known many things and would use this as a tool to make personal, parenting, and business decisions. I didn't, however, know where my future was going. That was the only thing I couldn't feel at all. As many healers and psychics say, their egos just won't let them see themselves.

I was also losing patience and faith by that point. I had been on my spiritual path for quite some time, working with many healers and devoting hundreds of hours to myself. Many of these healers and psychics had told me what I could and would do in the future, but nothing solid that I could see, or hear or touch was happening on Earth. I think I would have been fine if I had been told that no one would see my work in this lifetime. If that had been the case, I would have come to terms with it and lived my life that way. But I had always been told otherwise—I would make a big difference on this planet, and people would know about it. The 15 or so psychics I had seen by that point all said I would be speaking in front of hundreds, if not thousands, of people, improving both humanity and the Earth.

Deep within myself, I knew that I had accomplished something on the other side and that I was continuing to work every night, but I felt useless when I was awake. It was so cruel that I would do so much work—that my body would suffer for it—and that I would receive nothing in return. I felt like I was being punished. I didn't understand why it was happening to me. If the three, as well as Jerrest and Laneesh, kept saying that they were very happy with my work, then why wasn't anything else happening? I wasn't getting paid, nor was I getting any credit for my labors. Instead, I was becoming ill, and my body ached as though I were competing in triathlons during the night. I was sleeping terribly and would often wake up emotionally and physically exhausted. For nearly six months, I had to have massages every other day, and the therapist would ask me what I had done to my body. I had to just smile in response. What could I have said?

I continued to work with Kyle and Ellen, trying to see where I was going and how I could speed things up. Whenever Kyle saw me, there would be something new about my aura—something he had never seen before. When people were about to have major changes in life, Kyle would see tornadoes on top of their heads. This would be a sign that new people were coming or new projects were about to begin. At this point, I had several tornadoes on top of my head, so I knew some major changes were in the not-too-distant future. Just like my aura, these cyclones had aspects about them that were unlike anything Kyle had seen during his 30 years of readings. Some had colors in them, and others lightning. One looked like a lighthouse, sending its beam out. Kyle would often ask me if I felt dizzy, because he would feel this when he tried to tune into my energy. This was because I was vibrating much faster than anyone he had ever known. He said that my energy was like the center of a tornado itself.

Mako came to L.A. to do her healing sessions, and I saw her for the first time in almost a year. She came to my house to give me a session, and I was going to give her my healing in exchange.

"You look more like an alien than ever!" were her first words to me. I think it was a compliment that my energy wasn't like human beings' anymore. I hadn't told her much about my channeling or my experiences since I'd last seen her. During our session, she looked at my aura.

"You now have a deep blue light coming from your head," she said, "that goes all the way to another galaxy far away." I was glad that she could see what I had been hard at work on for months the previous year. She told me that I was going to channel a being and that she was afraid doing it would make my throat hurt. I knew immediately that she was talking about Prishnah. I then gave her my 30-second healing, and she was in shock. She said it was something very different from anything she'd experienced before, but it felt familiar at the same time, and she didn't quite understand what was happening. A few days later, I received an email from her. In it Mako said that her Earthly self didn't understand what I had done, but her other selves in other dimensions knew exactly what had happened, and that it was real and amazing. Though Mako was a powerful healer, my abilities were new territory for her, beyond anything she had ever experienced personally or observed in others.

In February, I took my daughter and her best friend to Hawaii. Before I went, I was told that, spiritually, this would also be an important trip. We arrived late at night, and the very next morning, I started to meditate. I went into a very deep state of meditation, and my entire body was vibrating. It was as though I had already been at a silent meditation retreat for five days. I started to speak to the three, but the language they were speaking was slightly different than those I normally spoke. I could tell that they were excited because their pitches were higher than usual, and they didn't want to stop. I called Kyle and asked him if I was going through some sort of transformation. When I had him listen to the recording I'd made of myself earlier, he said, "Oh my—they are merging." I meditated every day and was in a state of deep bliss. On the third day, I began to cry. The three were waiting for me to be awoken; they had suffered and sacrificed themselves. I realized that, up to this point, I had focused on my well-being. I was often very unhappy about why I was chosen and the sacrifices I had to make to accomplish my purpose. Then I realized that the three had been inside of me all along, being consious and watching what I went through my entire life without being able to say a word or help me. They must have felt very helpless. On top of that, they didn't know for sure if I would choose to follow my life purpose. I could have refused to continue my spiritual journey. They had no control over my decisions because of my free will. Even now, they could speak only when I let them, and they had no power or control over me. For the first time, I experienced deep compassion and gratitude for their trust in me and their patience. I forged a new kind of connection with this understanding.

When I returned from Hawaii, they told Kyle that the pipe they were in had opened up, and that they now had much more space. They said that Hawaii carried a special energy, and that I only accomplished what I had because I was there.

Even though the Hawaii experience was amazing and gratifying, I was still frustrated and lost. Both Ellen and Kyle said that my future partner would show up and that he would bring my work with him. At that time in my life, I hated the idea of needing someone else to complete me. Was I not enough? It felt like an insult. Why wasn't this guy showing up? Why was he taking forever? I was very angry with the three, with Jerrest, and with the whole world. I would often scream and cuss. I knew that being on a spiritual path could be long, difficult, and not rewarding in the traditional sense. In fact, Kyle and I would often say that it was easier not to know, or not to go on a spiritual journey at all. One cannot suffer from what one doesn't know. And once one started on a spiritual path, there was no ending. Both Kyle and I knew, however, that we were way past the point of no return. The only option was to keep going.

On other fronts, I had better news. Early in March, my daughter found out that she had been accepted to her first-choice school in Ojai. By August 30th, my daughter would be gone, and in a month my son would start to drive. It was the perfect time to begin my life's purpose full-time. Just when I was discussing with Kyle how my work was going to start, I got an email from Tim. He wrote that he had known for a while that I wanted to do spiritual work, and that he knew my heart was no longer in the furniture business. He said that, if I wanted to, I could leave the company and he would support my current lifestyle until my spiritual work began to make money. I couldn't believe my eyes. I jumped at the opportunity and replied to him right away. "Yes," I wrote. "I want to retire. Thank you for the offer!" I knew the Universe was behind his decision to show this generosity to me.

For the next six weeks, I was incredibly busy searching for my successor. In the end, I convinced Tim that Brad, from our Nashville store, would be the best choice. He was my only choice. We needed someone who was a team player, who was rational, and who could listen to everyone's opinion and then choose what was best for the company. It would take a mature person to do all this.

Akiko decided to leave with me, so Brad had until July, when Akiko left, to take over what she was doing and get everything under control. I had no time to spare. When Brad came to Los Angeles and spent two weeks with me, I felt very confident that he would do a wonderful job. He would be a great and considerate boss to everyone. There was a lot to go over, as there was just so much happening with all our stores, employees, and supply issues. I realized for the first time just how much energy I had been investing in the company. The other three key management people came to L.A., and we completed what I had set out to do before I left. I felt that the company was solid and that it would do well for many years to come.

On my last day, I wrote everyone a goodbye letter. Many managers sent me very sweet emails, thanking me and wishing me the best. It was a bittersweet moment. I had learned from past experiences that unless I closed a door, another wouldn't open. I couldn't start my life's purpose unless I had completely finished my work with the furniture company. I needed to put all my energy into what I had come to Earth for. I had been waiting for many years, and it was now my time.

When I woke up on May 1st, I was lighter and happier, as if all my burdens had been lifted from my shoulders. I'd started the furniture company when I was 21 years old. I had been carrying 24 stores and over 80 employees with me 24 hours a day, seven days a week. I hadn't realized how much it affected me until I finally let go. Now nothing was stopping me from moving forward to accomplish my life's purpose.

Chapter 9 Reflections

No one has told me that life is easy, but no one has ever told me that life is difficult, either. When I feel discouraged, I seek refuge in nature. Water always soothes my soul, and being in forests or on mountains gives me a sense of serenity. When I look at tall redwood trees or the ocean, I feel that my life and existence is very small compared to them; they offer perspective: my life problems are small in comparison. When I cannot go out into nature, I seek refuge in meditation. That I can do no matter where I am at or what time it is.

• • •

Variations of this meditation were taught to me by a few different teachers. This meditation is more advanced than meditation 1 but is a very effective soul and body cleanser. I do this meditation when I lose my center and want to connect to my soul. You might want to record the following meditation in your own voice first and play it while you meditate, as this is a guided meditation. Or you may choose to go to my website, www.astarchild.com, to listen to my recording of Guided Meditation 2

Guided Meditation 2 by Ariyana ~a star child~

(You might want to set the alarm for ten minutes or any length of time you wish to meditate.)

Close your eyes and relax your body. Take a few deep breaths in and out. As you breathe in, bring white light into your body. As you breathe out, let go of any stress or worries you are carrying with you. Let your body get used to the rhythm of your breath coming in and going out, and stay with it. Take another few breaths in and out. When you breathe in your next breath, fill your entire body with white light. Breathe out with all toxins you have in your body. Breathe in white light, and breathe out to cleanse your body. Take a few more breaths in and out. When you breathe in next time, breathe in white light to fill your heart. Breathe out from your heart. Breathe in and out a few more times to your heart. When your heart is full of white light, on your next exhale, imagine white light going down from your heart to the core of the Earth like a tree root. When it reaches the core, inhale the white light coming out of the core of the Earth straight up to your heart. Imagine a white tube connecting the heart and the core of the Earth. You exhale white light from your heart to the core of the Earth, and you inhale white light from the core of the Earth to your heart. Breathe in and out few more times. When you feel deeply connected to the Earth, bring your attention to the sun high above you in the sky. Breathe in and out and feel the warmth of the sun and its white heat coming down to your head. Take a few breaths in and out. On your next inhale, bring the white light straight down from the sun to your heart. On your next exhale, bring the white light straight up from your heart to the sun. Imagine a white tube connecting the sun to your heart. Inhale and exhale a few more times, imagining white light going up and down between the heart and the sun. Now put your attention back to your heart. Inhale the white light into your heart. On your next exhale, bring the white light from the heart down to the Earth. On your next inhale, white light goes straight from the core of the Earth all the way to the sun. On your next exhale, white light goes straight from the sun down to the center of the Earth. Imagine a white tube going into the ground as far as you can imagine and then up to the sky as far as you can imagine. Inhale and exhale a few more times. On your next breath, take your attention back to your heart. You inhale to your heart and exhale to expand the circle of light that includes the sun and the core of the Earth. You inhale and exhale the white light, and your heart becomes the center of the Universe. Inhale and exhale a few more times. Feel your connection to the Universe and Earth; you are the center of all things. Let go of your conscious breath and inhale and exhale naturally. You can continue to sit as long as you wish, or you can open your eyes and come back to your body.

What did you experience?

1._____
_____
2._____
_____
3._____
_____

CHAPTER 10

My Life's Purpose

The two most important days in your life are the day you are born and the day you find out why. – Mark Twain

For about a week after I left the furniture company, I just rested. I must say that I enjoyed the peace and the absence of drama. But at the same time I began to grow restless. I was a doer, and was happiest when I was accomplishing something. I also knew that I had "retired" from the business so that I could begin my true life's purpose—so that I could help the Earth and humanity. The three, Jerrest, and Laneesh were telling me that for months they had been preparing for me to start my work—work that went beyond opening the gateway to the galaxy that had occupied my nights—and I understood more than ever before that I'd needed to stop working at the furniture company, as it stole more of my energy than I'd ever realized. So I couldn't understand why, since I'd left my business, nothing was happening.

It was the middle of the day, and I was sitting outside beneath a pale blue sky and a shining sun when I rose and shouted up at the sky, and inwardly as well, "I quit!" The

Universe didn't respond, but I wasn't finished. "I've been on my spiritual path for over a decade, and I've got nothing to show for it. I'm not getting paid, I'm not getting any recognition, and I can't see that I've done anything." Though Kyle, Ellen, and the three kept reassuring me as to my accomplishments, at that moment I experienced a supreme sense of futility. The situation was no longer tolerable. In the past, no matter how hard the road had been, as long as I knew where I needed to go, I would always find ways of getting there. Up until that point, I'd always known what I'd wanted, and had almost always gotten it. I had always been in control. But with this Universal work, I had to wait for my life partner to show up, and I kept hearing that there was some more recalibration that needed to be done, as well as the alignment of other elements, before I could start my work. I had no control, and I couldn't keep my faith any longer.

Had I been dreaming? Were all the psychics I had seen wrong? Who was I to think that I was so special that I could change the world and the Universe? Was what I'd gone through in the last few years all in vain? I felt so depressed and lost. For the first time in a long time, I fell asleep crying that night.

The very next morning, I was in a different space. I was clear, focused, and refreshed. I had an epiphany: If the Universe wasn't going to help me take the next step, I would take it myself. I called Kyle.

"I need to start my work," I told him. "I am done waiting. There is no way that all the psychics I have seen and trust can see the same future, and it is just made up. If my guy is not coming, and the Universe is not bringing what it is supposed to, then I have no choice but to do this by myself. If Earth is not ready for me, and if nothing happens, at least I will know I did my best, and I will have no regrets."

Kyle and Ellen agreed with me. I brainstormed what I could do. I could set up a website, explaining why I was here, and posting all the messages from Prishnah, Kyrah, and Novysha. Or I could upload their light language messages onto YouTube. There were a few possibilities I could pursue, but I knew that beginning was very important.

I knew I had to bring information down from the other galaxy, so that Earth and humanity could make better decisions in order to have a brighter future. My time on this planet was limited—maybe another 40 years—so I knew I needed to move efficiently, so that I could make the biggest possible difference. I had to reach the most influential people and start with them. I could see myself working with CEOs and leaders of corporations, especially in the pharmaceutical, energy, environmental, government, and religious sectors. But how could I get to them? How could I make myself known? Then the answer came to me clearly. I needed to write a book. I needed to use it to tell the world who I was, why I was here, and that I was for real.

I made my decision to write a book on the 11th of May, 2014—it was Mother's Day. I am the type of person who, when I know what I want, starts moving forward no matter what. I had also received a clear message that I would write while my daughter was on a week long school trip to the East Coast, which began on the 28th of May. The next two weeks were frustrating. My ears were ringing like crazy, and I knew that the three were very happy that I would be writing a book very soon. Laneesh even said that he had a book of his own he wanted me to write. They had stopped me from working during the night so that my body would be more relaxed and I would have more energy. I knew that the three were working on the book during the next two weeks, readying the story for me. Kyle confirmed that Prishnah was showing up many nights, telling him what he wanted to say or showing him pages that he would then try and put in order.

On the morning of May 28th, I dropped my daughter at school at 5:00 a.m. to leave for her trip. My dog, Ren, was spending a week at his trainer's so that I could concentrate on writing my book. Right away, Kyle and I started to hear what the three and Laneesh had in mind for this project. That day, they told me what they wanted from it, its working title, and the number of chapters it would have, including each chapter's title and content. It was a good start.

After that, I was on fire. The next day, I began writing the first chapter. I would sit in the chair in front of my computer, writing one thought after another. In the next four days, I wrote six chapters, sometimes even writing through the night. This was surprising even to me, as I wasn't a writer and had never enjoyed it. But I knew I had to be the one to do it. Who else knew my life story exactly as it happened, and exactly how I felt? Kyle read some of my chapters, and he was quite impressed. I think I must have connected to some past life in which I had been a writer—it was coming so easily and naturally to me.

Just when I was about to finish Chapter 7, I received a message telling me I needed to stop. I felt that something was happening in Greece, and these events would change the ending of the book. I got confirmation of what I was feeling while having lunch with a girlfriend of mine who was Greek. She had just come back, in fact, from visiting her family in Greece. I was telling her that my daughter wanted to go back there for her summer vacation. Tim was taking our son to India for two weeks, so I had told my daughter that I would take her anywhere in the world. She wanted to go back there, and also to return to Santorini. As I enjoyed visiting new places, this was a bit surprising to me. I would have at least chosen another island. But she had insisted, so I gave in and made reservations. Then, at that lunch, my girlfriend told me that the Greeks believed that Atlantis was underneath Santorini. Oh my goodness! No wonder I was going back there. I knew I was going back to connect to the land, retrieve information, or open something inside me that was not yet unlocked.

For the previous few months, Jerrest had not been in my energy, and both Kyle and Ellen said that they hadn't seen him much either. This was new because Jerrest had been around me constantly since he'd arrived the previous June. When we asked Prishnah about this, he replied that Jerrest had been busy. By that point, I knew instinctively that Novysha and Jerrest were partners. Could Jerrest be my partner in this life? I wondered. But he was a spirit, and not in a human body. These thoughts had run through my mind during the preceding six months, but how could it have been possible? No matter what was happening, I knew that the time was close to when everything would unfold.

On the 3rd of June, 2014, I was channeling Prishnah, and Kyle was translating for me. We were trying to understand why they are here and why I was the one they chose. This is the message I received:

...

We—Prishnah, Kyrah, and Novysha—come from a planet just outside the three stars of Orion's Belt. According to your knowledge on the Earth, this planet is considered to be a star. You call us Betelgeuse, and Jerrest is from Supergiant. We are a very technically advanced society, with many characteristics similar to Earth's humans in terms of family and how we are raised. I, Prishnah, am the father and the leader of the seventh dimension of the Federation of the Light. Kyrah and Novysha are my twin daughters. Novysha is more like me, and one day in the future will be the leader of the Federation.

In a time of great strife, my planet had gone too far. Groups who held power didn't communicate with each other, and they were becoming greedy. They began destroying each other, searching to be the most powerful, which is not much different than your planet. Technology was used against us, and that is what I am afraid is happening on your planet as well. During this time, there was a handful of us from the Federation who were trying to convince everyone of what was going on and trying to change the direction of where they were heading. But we were too late. And the disaster was inevitable.

Our planet is parallel with the Earth. In this parallel Universe, we are one—the same planet in different dimensions. Earth is currently heading toward a similar downfall. We have come from the future into your present, which is our past, in the hope of making a difference and changing our future and yours.

Novysha volunteered to come to Earth and be born as a human being with no knowledge of her background. That's how Ariyana was born on August 5, 1971. The information was crystallized and formatted into the cells of Ariyana, and once it started to open, unlimited information began to flow. The information is not limited to my planet, or Earth, but includes all universal knowledge. This information lay dormant until Ariyana was strong and mature enough to be able to hold the total amount of it, and only if she chose to do so.

We have the ability to see the future of the Earth three years in advance. It is our intention to bring only information that is helpful and useful for humans and Earth through Ariyana.

• • •

It was a shocking revelation. Even though I was aware of some of this previously, Prishnah's formal announcement in this setting touched me deeply. It helped me grasp the reality of their existence as well my own—why I had returned to stars when I re-experienced my past lives. Prishnah's statement also helped me fully appreciate the gravity of the task before me. I had to take a few deep breaths before I could accept his words into my whole body and consciousness.

Chapter 10 Reflections

We are here on this Earth for many different reasons. Our life lessons and life purposes are unique to each individual. However, I believe that one fundamental truth we all live by is the same. That truth is that we are made out of love; that is our nature, our core, and our essence. Love is simply the most important force in us, and we can all connect to that. That is our birthright, and we should embrace it and live from that understanding every day.

Think of three people or things you love who make you smile just by thinking about them.

1._____
_____

2._____
_____

3._____
_____

How do you feel when you are thinking about them?

1._____
_____

2._____

_____

3._____

_____

Can you write three things that you admire and love about yourself?

1._____

_____

2._____

_____

3._____

_____

Close your eyes, and take a deep breath. Open your eyes, and read the questions and the answers you have given. Take another deep breath, and tell yourself, "I love you, you are enough, and I will take care of you." Take another deep breath, and tell yourself, "You are lovable, you are loving, and you are loved." Take another deep breath, and tell yourself, "I love you, and I know you are doing your best, and I am proud of you." Take another deep breath, and remember how you feel at this moment. Be kind to yourself. That is the key to open your heart and soul.

CHAPTER 11

Facing My Destiny

I have been impressed with the urgency of doing. Knowing is not enough; we must apply. Being willing is not enough; we must do. – Leonardo da Vinci

On the 8th of June, 2014, I woke up in the middle of the night, feeling the presence of someone in my bedroom. On the left side of the bed, a Greek god appeared, or at least that was my first impression. Tall, blonde, and muscular, the man offered me a charming smile and stared into my eyes with passion. I experienced almost exactly the same feeling I did when I'd seen my guardian angel. I was fully awake, but, at the same time, the person beside me was not real. I knew right away that it was Jerrest in a human body.

"Are you Jerrest?" I asked. He smiled and then disappeared. My heart was rushing. Jerrest had appeared, showing me what he would look like! I had been waiting for that sign for two years, and finally it had come.

First thing the next morning, I called Kyle. By tuning into my energy, he was able to see what I had seen.

"Oh, my God. He is very good-looking," Kyle said. "Yes, it has to be Jerrest." This made all the sense in the world.

Since the previous February, both Kyle and Ellen had experienced difficulty in making contact with Jerrest. He would show up, but then when we'd ask to speak to him, he wouldn't be around the way he used to. All of that time, he must have been preparing to awaken in a human body. For a while, Kyle and Ellen had felt that my future partner would be a very spiritual person, and that he was already in communication with Prishnah. I'd always wondered how this chosen person would manage to be so successful, handsome, and yet spiritual at the same time. I felt that the prospect or the promise was too good to be true. But if I'd seen the human embodiment of Jerrest, then anything was possible.

Kyle and I asked Prishnah if it was in fact Jerrest who had appeared to me the night before.

"I am very sorry that I couldn't have told you this before," said Prishnah. "We had a contract that if you attained a certain consciousness level, the next door would open. We didn't know if you would get here, where Jerrest could be awoken. Even though you volunteered to do the work, you always had free will, and we could not control your decisions." I was happy and at the same time, quite angry. They, especially Jerrest, had known all along that he would be my partner, but they had pretended that someone else would be coming very soon.

"Jerrest is in love with you," Ellen used to say. "And I think he is blocking you from meeting your partner." I'd thought that if this were true, it might be because Jerrest was jealous, as he was meant to be my future partner in another dimension. I told Kyle that I couldn't make sense of it. If Jerrest loved me so much, then why wouldn't he want me to have someone in my life until he arrived? Why wouldn't he want me to be happy in the present if he knew he wouldn't be coming into my life for another year?

"It's a male thing," Kyle said. "He didn't want to share you." Whether Kyle was right or not, I couldn't agree with what Jerrest had done, and I was quite upset.

The next day, the three told Kyle that Jerrest had left a message for me. "My dearest," he'd said, "I will be there very soon." The three told me that Jerrest would make up for everything he had done and that he would make me very happy. Then, after the 8th of June, Kyle and Ellen were no longer able to communicate with Jerrest. Ordinarily, Kyle was able to find anyone—living or deceased, in this world or another dimension—and speak with that person, so he found the situation to be very odd. But at least we no longer had to wonder how or where my partner would arrive to help me with my life's purpose. Jerrest had not only been with me every day for the past year, but through all of this human life, and possibly many more. I felt relieved. I had been living a life of solitude and was dreading the idea of getting to know my new partner when he arrived. Based on my previous experiences, I knew it would take me a long time to get to know someone. Given that I was trying to save the world, I lacked that time. I was also not looking forward to the mundane process of getting to know this partner, as well as his friends and his family members.

But if it was Jerrest, it wouldn't require that time, and I wouldn't have to say or explain anything to him.

All along, Kyle had said that my life partner was my twin flame. Twin flames are couples who spend an entire lifetime together happily, and then want to spend another lifetime together again. My understanding was that a person had a soul family, which came to Earth again and again, playing different roles each time. These were called soul mates. Some might have two or three soul mates in a lifetime, and some might have ten. One is incredibly lucky to have a soul mate as one's life partner, as it is very rare, but having a twin flame as a life partner is even rarer! The only thing more rare than this is having one's twin soul as a life partner. A twin soul is one's counterpart, and they share the same soul or source. When one first comes to Earth, the soul splits into two parts—male and female—so that it can maximize its learning experiences. It is more likely than not that one's twin soul will not inhabit the Earth at the same time he or she does. One's twin soul could be in a different part of the world—or in a different age—and one might never glimpse him or her. You can see why it is almost impossible or unheard of to have your twin soul as your partner. I had been told, however, that when one meets a twin flame or a twin soul, a sort of understanding, connection, and recognition passes between them that transcends how couples normally relate.

As I was processing this information about Jerrest, I was also embarking on the trip to Greece with my daughter after she graduated from middle school. For me, returning to

Santorini felt like going home. I stopped by a crystal shop in Oia that I had visited two years before and picked up a pyramid of agate and a sphere of ametrine, both of which were very powerful stones. I meditated daily and soaked in the Mediterranean Sea. My ears were ringing like crazy most of the nights while I was in Santorini, and I sensed I was connecting to the land and my past lives. During the night, I believed I was receiving information as I slept and that was what had brought me back to Greece.

It was also the perfect vacation for my daughter and me. While we were there, we met up with some friends in Athens, and I fell in love with Greece and Greek people all over again. The scenic beauty and energy of the country, and the kindness and generosity of its people, made Greece one of my favorite countries in the world.

When I came back to Los Angeles, I felt stronger and more centered. I met up with Kyle, and he checked my energy.

"You are inside the brightest golden light I have ever seen," he said. We asked the three about it, and they said that the light was for Jerrest to find me by. I was still in doubt, and worried that he had forgotten how to find me. The three said that my golden light went straight up into the sky for many miles, so that any angelic being could locate me. Still, I was not convinced. I had felt that Jerrest would find me in Greece.

"You are correct," the three said. "Your intuition is right on. Jerrest, however, is behind schedule." How could he be behind schedule? I wondered. He'd literally had all the time in the world to prepare for this moment. But they confirmed that my Greece trip had still been a valuable one. I had connected to past lives there, in which I used to teach.

I was impatient by that point. If Jerrest was able to appear in front of me three weeks before, why hadn't he done it again? Or why hadn't he sent me a message through my dreams, or through Kyle, or something? I asked both Kyle and Ellen to look into Jerrest's whereabouts. They both saw him in a hospital bed, wrapped like an Egyptian mummy. He had broken bones and was unable to walk. It seemed he must have had a major accident. Kyle and Ellen said that he was in a lot of pain, and that he was more upset than I was over not being able to come to me.

I asked the three why, if Jerrest was "here," he wasn't doing the work instead of me. He was connected, after all. They said that, this time around, the work had to be done by a female. Through the history of humanity, females had ruled more prosperously and more harmoniously. A woman's energy was now needed to make the necessary changes. I had heard that in Egypt there had once been a female ruler who had managed to achieve more prosperity than any other ruler. One day, however, she disappeared, and everything she'd built was destroyed, as if she'd never existed at all. I thought it was time for us to acknowledge the fact that a woman could once again be the key to our future. Mother energy is connected to nature and to the core of all creation, so a woman could govern without being hindered by her ego.

Even though I was frustrated with my progress, I had been receiving confirmations through my dreams, and from

Kyle. Ever since I'd found out about Jerrest's accident, and since I'd learned that he needed to finish his recalibration before he could find me, I had been sending Jerrest healing. One night, he came into my dreams and held me in his arms. I could definitely feel him and knew that our time to be together again was close. I had been going through another round of recalibration, and neither Kyle nor I were feeling very well. Our ears were ringing day and night; I was having headaches, and Kyle was experiencing cold symptoms. One morning, I sat and sent Jerrest a healing. Then I sent a healing to Kyle.

I would sit and meditate slightly to center myself. I would take a deep breath and connect myself to ALL. Then I would set my intention to send a healing to a certain person and would let the three come out. They would speak for about 30 seconds, and I would move my hands according to their sounds to work on the universal grid.

"Do you remember that crystal you gave me?" Kyle asked the next day. "At 9:00 a.m. yesterday, bright blue light started to shine out of it. I thought you might have been meditating or something. It was really cool." I explained to Kyle that I had been sending healing to him at that very time. The crystal he was referring to was one of the 36 I had programmed to open the gate to a new galaxy. So far, I had given crystals to Kyle, Akiko, my son, and my daughter. I was told that I would give the rest of the 32 crystals to people around the world, all of whom would help me with my life's purpose. I knew that, through these crystals, I would be able to immediately connect with the people who were in possession of them, no matter where they were.

• • •

A week after I returned from Greece, I found I was getting more upset with each passing day. I had been told that something big would happen while I was on my trip, and that I couldn't work on my book until I'd come back. But to me, it didn't seem that anything major had happened. Yet again, I was left waiting. I also felt I couldn't finish my book until I'd met Jerrest and gotten his input. The three insisted, however, that it was my project and that they didn't want Jerrest to interfere with it.

"If I really am the savior of the world," I told the three, "and am going to do all the things you guys say I am, how the hell do I have the power to do all that's expected of me? And how can I trust you if you can't even make Jerrest find me?" I was incredibly frustrated. Everything seemed impossible, and I felt powerless and useless.

"Well, you have been doing this for a long, long time," Prishnah said. "It has always been you and Jerrest. You are the Archangel Gabriel, and Jerrest is the Archangel Michael. You two have brought messages to humanity throughout history. You have been changing the course of humankind by coming down to Earth and playing the roles of key historic figures again and again."

As I listened to Prishnah, I struggled to maintain my grip on reality. To be told that I was the Archangel Gabriel was akin to being told that I was Jesus Christ or Buddha—a totemic figure who dwarfed my self-perception. I had known that my soul came from a very high dimension, and that almost none of the other beings there would come down to Earth. There was nothing but oneness where I'd descended from, but I enjoyed being on Earth because of its beauty and the individuality I was able to experience. But I hadn't seen Prishnah's declaration coming. I knew the Archangel Gabriel had come to Earth in the form of Noah and other important figures. It took two weeks for me to really internalize what this information meant to my mission and to me. I told myself that whether I was Gabriel or not wasn't important. What was most important was doing what I'd come to do. If being Gabriel would help me accomplish it, then so be it.

The three and Laneesh offered more explanations as to why I was here. The creators and beings of the higher dimensions were unhappy with what had been happening on Earth. They had lost almost all hope for the continuation of humanity. They told me that I was the only one who had said there was still hope, and that I would come to work with the humans. I was thankful that those in the higher dimensions gave me this one last chance. I was also grateful that Jerrest had agreed to come with me and help. I couldn't wait to be united with him again. And I was also appreciative of all the people and entities who had supported me—who had made me who I was.

My mission was huge. I had come to change the consciousness of humanity. As Ariyana—my star identity—in a human body, I couldn't say with certainty that I would be able to accomplish what I came for, but I would do my best to make the changes I could and to be of service to humanity and to the Earth. This was my commitment and my promise. I knew there were many beings of light on Earth in human form, and they had come to help make a difference. I knew they would find me and work with me. What we were trying to do was very difficult and very time-consuming. The massive shift we were toiling for couldn't be accomplished overnight. It would take decades, or possibly longer. It might not even be completed in my lifetime. It was, however, crucial that we began *now*. I knew from my 40 years' experience as a human that, individually, we are weak; but, when people come together in community for a common cause, they can move mountains. I looked forward to working with the light beings I knew were on Earth, those in different dimensions, and any other being who would stand up with me to save the Earth and humanity.

Chapter 11 Reflections

I am very honored and humbled because my life purpose is to help humanity, Earth, and the Universe at large. But I am well aware that I have lived many past lives, learning other simple lessons about love, money, power, relationships, etc. One life purpose is not better or worse than another. It just is. Let go of your judgmental mind, because your soul knows exactly what you need to do in this life and is with you every step of the way. Since most of us don't know why we are here, talk to your heart and see what it desires to do in this life.

What are the three things you care about most and want to accomplish in this life?

1._____
_____

2._____
_____

3._____
_____

How would you feel if you could accomplish them?

1. _____
_____
2. _____
_____
3. _____
_____

What are the first steps you could take to make your dreams reality?

1. _____
_____
2. _____
_____
3. _____
_____

Close your eyes, and take a deep breath. Open your eyes, and read the questions and the answers you have given. Take another deep breath, and say out loud, "I am going to do my best to accomplish [your answers to the first question]." Take another deep breath, and do the second and the third answers. Take another deep breath, and close your eyes. Imagine that you are actually accomplishing your dreams one by one. When you open your eyes, remember how you felt when you were accomplishing your heart's desire.

CHAPTER 12

Coming Home

Believe in yourself! Have faith in your abilities! Without a humble but reasonable confidence in your own powers you cannot be successful or happy. – Norman Vincent Peale

Mount Shasta had been on my mind for several months, and I felt that it would be good to visit it before my book was finished. I decided to go for my birthday, and Kyle agreed to come with me. While I was doing some online research about things to do in Mount Shasta, my entire being began to vibrate, and I knew I was doing the right thing. I felt that the three and Laneesh were very happy that I was going.

It's a nine-hour drive to Mount Shasta, and, during it, the three and Laneesh gave Kyle and me information regarding my concerns and expectations about the trip and my future work. At that point, Kyle was the only person who could translate their light languages, which concerned me. What if something happened to Kyle? The three and Laneesh confirmed that my son also had the ability to translate their languages, but he was only 16 years old, and he also had free will. They also told me that, eventually, I would have a trinity of translators, and that the third would be a young female. This young woman would be someone I would enjoy traveling with, and we would become good friends. I was also informed that I would receive an infusion of energy, and I would have dreams about the future during the trip. Laneesh said that he had left the windows and doors of Mount Shasta unlocked so that I could open them while I was there. Everyone was very excited that we were on our way!

As predicted, about 15 minutes before the Mount Shasta exit on the freeway, I started to feel a surge of energy throughout my body. It was warm and strong, and I was vibrating with it. My ears began ringing loudly as well. I looked at Kyle.

"Do you feel this?" I asked.

"Yeah," he replied. "It just started. It's incredible, isn't it?" We knew we had arrived. Kyrah and Novysha jumped out and began to speak.

"Welcome home!" Kyrah said.

We checked into our two-bedroom cabin on the lake, and suddenly I was exhausted. The vibrations I'd felt earlier had dissipated somewhat, but my ears were still ringing. I was told that the entirety of Mount Shasta was a vortex, and that the city was inside it. Within this great vortex, there were also smaller vortices scattered about. My ears would ring when there was a difference in frequencies, altering me to different vortical or dimensional openings. My body was exhausted, but my emotions were running high, and it took me a long while to fall asleep. That night was filled with thunder, lightning, and fierce rain.

I woke up the next morning ready to receive whatever I was supposed to from Mount Shasta. It was my birthday, and I felt that something amazing would happen to me on that day. My first step was to meditate inside the "pyramid." I had discovered this pyramid by accident when I was searching for things to do online. A healer had built the pyramid by channeling beings from other dimensions, and a person can now rent it by the hour. I knew immediately that I needed to go there. When I arrived at the site, the land was so powerful that I felt my own energy going down into the ground, like the stretching, reaching roots of a tree. I moved through a tunnel, walked up a few steps, and entered through a trap door. When I walked inside the pyramid, I noticed that the 15-foot-high structure lacked any doors or windows and had a copper and quartz crystal "roof." Its pyramid shape was supposed to heighten existing energy, but my first reaction was that my ears began ringing, and I wasn't sure if I'd actually be able to stay there for a full hour. Inside, it was dark, but my eyes soon adjusted, and I became aware of my surroundings as I sat on a meditation cushion in the middle of the room. I began to meditate, and within a few minutes Kyrah and Novysha came, and they began to speak. I sent myself a healing, asking that I receive everything I was supposed to while I was there.

Within five minutes of being alone inside the pyramid, I wasn't able to sit up. I moved one of the nearby futons to the center of the room, lay down, and closed my eyes. The intense flow of energy dissolved my body, and I disappeared. Or rather, I began to merge with everything that existed. In pure bliss, as if I had been meditating for five days straight, I experienced oneness. After about 30 minutes in this transcendent state, I felt complete, and I sat up. I emerged from the pyramid contented and renewed. Afterward, I drove back to the cabin to meet up with Kyle.

"Wow," he said, staring at me. "You look different." I told him about my experience in the pyramid. I asked Kyle to ask the three and Laneesh what had actually happened to me. They said that I had dissolved into electrons and small particles, and that they had polished each piece and then put me back together. I had been cleansed, and the pyramid—small and contained—had been a safe space in which to do it. Kyle said that since the energy had been so amplified there, even someone without any spiritual experience would feel something. Someone as sensitive as I was would simply disappear and become one with it all.

Kyle said that he had woken up in the middle of the night and had tuned into my energy in order to check it. He told me that he felt as if he were in the middle of a tornado, which he had said before in the past, and that, wherever I went, I was existing in the midst of my own vortex. The energy had been spinning, and he had become so hot that he'd needed to step outside the bedroom to cool down. When he went into the living room, he saw a giant, hairy being sitting there. He was so scared! Kyle asked who this being was, but he only sat quietly on the sofa. When Kyle told me of this, I guessed I had gained another spiritual guide.

That day, Kyle and I met with Kevin, our hiking guide, and drove up the mountain together. Shortly after we started, my ears, as well as Kyle's, began to ring. We asked Kevin if he knew if there was anything special around that area, and he said that he didn't. After making several more turns, the ringing in our ears grew so loud that Kyle and I asked Kevin to stop the car. He pulled over in a small outlook area. We got out of the car and found ourselves walking in the same direction, toward some rocks and trees. After finding spots to sit down, we began meditating. I asked Kyle what he saw, and he said that the space between the two trees behind me was getting foggy. This meant a doorway was opening up.

After the fog cleared, Kyle could see a giant crystal. I asked Kyle if he could see anything else, and he said that he would go inside and find out. He walked into the crystal, and saw a beautiful woman in ornate clothing. The woman said that she would take us to the entrance of Antaros, but, before we could go through, she would need to see our passes. According to her, Antaros was the name of the fifth-dimensional city beneath where we were sitting. The only people who were allowed to go down were the ones who held passes, which were engraved on a person's palm. After she looked into our palms, she agreed to take us down to the city. When we arrived at the entrance, Kyle saw four strong-looking men there. The four had dark skin, and their black hair was tied in ponytails. They appeared as though they could have been

Hawaiian, but they seemed like statues who had come to life to guard the city.

When we walked into the city, Kyle beheld something from a fairytale. The sky was startlingly blue, and the people, too, blazed with beauty. Some, but not all, were exceptionally tall, with blond hair and blue eyes, and looked very different from the guards we'd seen earlier. We arrived at the city, and it reminded us of a Renaissance Faire. Kyle saw a farmers' market, where people were selling animals, fruits, and other goods. Everyone seemed very happy, and the children were playing. One of them—a little girl—looked at Kyle, and waved for him to follow her.

Kyle followed, and the next thing we knew, we were inside an exquisite building. The little girl had changed into elaborate clothing, put on makeup, and was sitting on an altar.

"You are supposed to pick up your belongings from the past," she said to me. "It is very important that you collect what you came here for." There were many items laid out on the floor before the girl. From these objects, I took a key and a white box, which Kyle asked me to open. Inside, there was a paper with ornate writing on it that I didn't recognize. Immediately, Kyle realized that the little girl and I were looking at the paper in the same way. The mirror images stayed with Kyle and proved to be significant.

Everyone seemed to be pleased with what I had chosen, and Kyle and I came back into our bodies. We then continued to drive up the mountain to the place where another doorway to the city of Lemuria existed. It was the same place where, three years ago, I had met my family for the first time. That time, however, I hadn't actually made it to the city of Telos, as I was taken to another dimension and to a spaceship instead. The doorway before Kyle and me now didn't feel as strong as the one we'd just come from. Perhaps, we thought, it had been used by too many people and lost its magic.

Still, Kyle and I closed our eyes and began meditating. Two of the four guards we saw earlier returned; they guarded all doorways to Lemuria. They motioned us that we could pass, so Kyle and I went down the transparent elevator beneath Mount Shasta. When we arrived, we were on a big city street. What we saw was very similar to earlier, in Antaros, and it felt intensely familiar. Then we stopped in front of a gate to a home. We realized that it was a place I had lived before. We went throught the gate and walked down a long corridor. No glass windows existed anywhere. The house was open-aired, with marble floors, plaster walls, and many pillars. The furniture that we passed was covered with cloth, as if no one had lived there for a while. A painting on the wall caught my eye—it featured a man, a woman, and a child, and Kyle knew immediately that I was the adult female in that painting. We felt complete and decided to leave Lemuria. When we opened our eyes, we were back at the big clearing on Mount Shasta.

• • •

When I came back into my body, I asked the three and Laneesh if I had done what I'd needed to do on the mountain, and they said yes. I also asked why I was there. The answer I received was that I'd come to Mount Shasta to open my sight—my third eye, or the eye to the soul. And, feeling satisfied, I came down from the mountain.

That night, while I was having dinner with Kyle, I had to ask where Jerrest was.

"There's no excuse for him not showing up for my birthday," I said. But then he appeared in spirit form in front of Kyle. He was holding a cupcake with a candle. Kyle told Jerrest that it wasn't the sort of cupcake I liked—I liked everything chocolate. Jerrest explained by saying he was colorblind. OK, he had made me laugh. I asked why he hadn't come in person, and he answered that he was still very fragile. While I wasn't happy with his answer, I also wasn't going to let him ruin my birthday. That night, I slept deeply.

I woke up early the next morning. I knew that I needed to go back to the mountain to meditate and process what I had gone through the day before. It took me almost 40 minutes to get from my cabin to the end of the road. Where the altitude reached 7,770 feet, I stopped in a small parking lot. Kevin had told us that the Native Americans who lived there considered that area to be the most powerful. I parked my car and walked until I found a space where I could be alone and sit among the trees. For a while, I sat, and then I recorded what the three and Laneesh wanted to say. Afterwards, I felt content, and once again, came down the mountain. Though some times it was louder than at others, my ears were ringing almost all the time, and I felt that my visit to Mount Shasta was complete. I also felt that might be my last physical journey there.

I came back to the cabin and asked Kyle to translate the light language. In the message, Novysha had said that I should remember that I was more powerful than I probably thought—I could control the doors and windows to any dimension. Novysha also said that I didn't need Jerrest to do what I'd come to do, and that we both had counterparts: Hope and Faith. Kyrah said that they all loved me very much. Prishnah said that I should engage in my power and that I had the ability to go through windows and doors to other dimensions. I was ready. Laneesh, who has two bodies, one in the past and one simultaneously in the present, said that we made a trinity, and that Novysha, Prishnah, and Kyrah made one as well.

Many signs in Mount Shasta read "Shasta-Trinity National Forest." It seemed trinities were following me wherever I went. When I spoke with Heidi, the woman who made the DNA activation art, I asked her about designing a company logo for me, which I might be able to use as the cover of this book. I told her that I wanted the logo to feature the symbol of a trinity.

During our time at Mount Shasta, I absorbed a rush of love and appreciation from the three and Laneesh. At the same time, however, a sense of great responsibility took hold, as I knew I was ready to begin my work. Whenever I was going through a major transformation, water—whether it be a natural hot spring, lake, river, ocean, or even a bathtub—always comforted my body and soul. I was so close to that element. So, while we were on our trip, Kyle and I went to the Stewart Mineral Springs Retreat to soothe our bodies.

When we retuned to Mount Shasta that night, my ears were ringing loudly. I assumed that some sort of recalibration was happening with my body. Then, on our drive home to Los Angeles, I gained some major insight into the current situation. The original plan did not involve Jerrest coming to Earth to help me. Kyle had explained to me that Jerrest was against my (Novysha) coming to Earth. But I did it anyway, exercising my free will.

Kyle had detailed how I (Novysha) volunteered to come to the Earth. I was attending a Galactic Federation meeting (with over 500 beings there). Prishnah was the speaker of the house, and he was asking for volunteers. I raised my hand. He ignored me initially, since he didn't think I should go, but I was insistent. Jerrest was sitting next to me, and he was very upset, telling me not to go. I also felt that, if he was planning to come help me, he should have been already in my life like my children, my sister, or Kyle, who played important roles in my awakening. So, as I was driving in L.A., I put two and two together and understood that Jerrest was not part of the plan, at least not the original one.

This was my journey, not his. But, after seeing me with other men, Jerrest became too jealous, so he changed his mind, and decided that he would come down to be my hero. He had been influencing all my psychics, and even fooling the angels, so that they would tell me that I needed my life partner to start my work, and that he was just around the corner. The three and Laneesh, my guides and angels, as well as Kyle and Ellen, had all been very upset with him. "How could Jerrest have abused his power?", they would ask. Why would he have delayed the plans and allowed me to go through so much unnecessary suffering?

When I asked the three and Laneesh why Jerrest still hadn't shown up, they said that he underestimated the recalibration I had gone through, and it was taking him much longer than he had anticipated to ready himself to meet me.

"Why wouldn't Jerrest just show up and go through his recalibration next to me?" I asked them. "That way, I could help him, as I went through the same thing. And I could also give him healing and support."

"As you are aware," they said, "beings of light know your plans, but at the same time, beings with not-so-good intentions also know that you are coming. You are strong enough now that no one can hurt you. You are not, however, strong enough to protect Jerrest if he is not in possession of his full power. It is crucial that he goes through his own recalibration and shows up when he is ready."

At this point, I reflected on everything that had led me to my purpose. It was becoming clear that I had been operating with incomplete and occasionally confusing information. Looking back, I wouldn't change anything about my past, but I know my journey would have been easier with more accurate guidance. I wish that three years ago someone had told me that I would go through a rapid, intense period of spiritual growth, and that during that period, my recalibration would be difficult, I wouldn't have much of a social life, and I wouldn't have a partner, because I didn't have the extra energy to share with others. I also wish I had known that my work would not start until my recalibration was complete and all the other pieces were in place—and that those pieces included all the people who would help me on my journey. I came to understand that I am perpetually ahead of schedule, and that I needed to wait for others to catch up to me. I also had to be patient and wait for conditions on Earth to be right for me to emerge and fulfill my purpose. Earlier in my journey, however, I had been told repeatedly that my life's purpose and my life partner were just around the corner.

With hindsight, I understand that they were afraid that if they had told me the truth, I would have grown discouraged and quit. For the previous three years, I'd always been waiting for something to happen and failed to be present in the moment. I had experienced feelings of powerlessness, intense frustration, disappointment, and anger.

But I am here today, and I am much stronger, more present, and feel more compassion for others' suffering. I learned firsthand that sometimes a person doesn't have control over a situation, but if he or she keeps moving forward, a door will open, no matter how difficult things have become. I know now that the answer is not to wait for the future, or things, or even a partner to save me, because I am whole just as I am, and I am the only one responsible for my life. I had experienced exactly the journey I'd needed in order for my soul to learn and expand.

I still long to be in a loving relationship, because I firmly believe that we humans can achieve more, and enjoy the highest love, through sharing our lives with a partner. I love being in love—being loved by someone else and loving my partner in return. I can't imagine *not* sharing my life with someone I love. I do look forward to one day meeting a partner who is compatible with me on many levels, and whose heart is open, wanting to serve and help the Earth and humanity. Now, I don't know if that person will be Jerrest, or someone I've never met before. I do know, however, that the right person will come into my life and that my doors and heart are open to all possibilities.

Kyle and I discussed what Novysha had said about Hope and Faith. In a book about angels, I had once read that Gabriel had a female counterpart named Hope, and that Michael had one named Faith. So who was my counterpart? For a long time, I thought Jerrest was my counterpart, but we didn't share the same soul, and were very different—opposite in many ways. Then I realized the truth. My twin soul—my counterpart—was my son! It made all the sense in the world, and at the same time it was extremely shocking. After all, the odds of meeting your twin soul on Earth are extremely low. That my twin soul was actually someone I had known and loved for much of my adult life was completely unexpected.

I had always wondered why my son and I were so similar, including the movies and food we liked and even how we thought. We could talk about anything—including all things spiritual—and we possessed the same understanding of how life worked. Many psychics I had seen had pointed out the strong connection between the two of us and how we could communciate through telepathy. Now, it all made sense. But I could only see it once I was able to let go of the belief that I needed Jerrest to complete me and Jerrest wasn't my twin soul. In the past, the three had told me that if I decided not to do my work, the only other person on this Earth who could do it was my son. But they had wanted a female this time around. While Kyle and I were discussing this in the car, he saw a box in front of me. It was the same box that sat in the back of my neck, the same one that had appeared when I'd started channeling light languages. I assumed that this box would move either to my son's neck or to that of the third translator, who would be showing up very soon, and belong to her. It was a breakthrough. The three told Kyle that, after our trip to Mount Shasta, he would be able to translate their light languages fluently into English. Kyle thought that, after the box was set in my son or the third translator, he would be able to connect the box, and its bearer would hear my light languages in English. This prospect excited both Kyle and me.

I asked Kyle to confer with the three and clarify whether or not the little girl we saw in Antaros was me and, if so, what her role was there. Kyle told me he believed that she was me and thought that she was the oracle of the city.

"She is the seer and the holder of the light," Prishnah said. "And you are the young child in that dimension." He also told me that the new guide who had appeared in Mount Shasta was a protector from my life in Lemuria. Now, as I was ready to use my full power on Earth, the protector had been given to me once again. From that point on, he would go with me wherever I went, and serve as my guard.

My trip to Mount Shasta was invaluable, and there was no doubt in my mind that it was a part of my destiny. Without the experiences and realizations I had there, I couldn't have finished my book or started my work. Since my return, Kyle has noticed that my energy has shifted completely, because *this is my time*.

Chapter 12 Reflections

We are in control of our lives even though we don't feel as if we are. We were taught to live in certain ways and follow certain rules because, if we don't, we won't be loved or will be punished. However, that is not the reality of things. There are no formulas or set rules that will guarantee your happiness in life. You are the only one who can create the life you want and who is responsible for your own life. Take responsibility for your actions and take control of your life, because that is the way to live from your heart and soul. What is best for you is usually what is best for others around you, because you are living from your truth. The highest action we can take is to serve the happiness of others. Take a deep breath, and find trust in yourself, your heart, and your soul. These are the parts of yourself that know what is best for you.

What are the three things that can enrich your life that you haven't given yourself the permission to act upon?

1._____

_____

2._____

_____

3._____

_____

How would your actions affect people or things around you if you gave yourself permission?

1._____

2._____

3._____

Can you find creative solutions so you can enrich your life and also improve others' lives?

1._____

2._____

3._____

Close your eyes, and take a deep breath. Open your eyes, and read the questions and the answers you have given. Take another deep breath, and tell yourself, "I love you, and I trust you. I can contribute." Take another deep breath, and close your eyes. Imagine that you are making positive changes in your life and also see others around you happy. When you open your eyes, remember how you felt when you were making yourself and others happy.

I woke up standing next to the sealed sarcophagus and realized that I was back inside the closed pyramid. I ran my hands up and down the stone tomb and could feel the writings and drawings carved into it. On the top panel, I felt the shape of an eye with a sun in the middle. This is a sarcophagus of the Sun God Ra. I must be the wife of Ra in this lifetime. Using all my might, I pushed the sarcophagus open. As I looked inside, I saw a dead body with a golden animal mask on its head. Reaching down, I removed it. The mask was so heavy. Then, to my complete disbelief, the face before me was my own. Am I Ra, or am I his wife? Or could I be both? Before I could emerge from my shock and confusion, white light began radiating between my eyes and eyes of the dead body, blinding me. It turned into a giant sphere of energy, growing larger and larger until it enveloped us both. Our bodies merged with this light and became one. The light became stronger, and then it began to rise.

I could see three pyramids below me, and, above me, three stars in the same formation. There were beams of white light between the pyramids and the stars. I was inside the light, ascending into the sky.

PART III

Future

CHAPTER 13

Walking Your Path Without Judgment

Too often we underestimate the power of a touch, a smile, a kind word, a listening ear, an honest compliment, or the smallest act of caring, all of which have the potential to turn a life around. – Leo Buscaglia

I've gone through a long, difficult, and intense spiritual journey with the help of many healers, psychics, teachers, and my angels. What I am going to share in this chapter is the accumulated wisdom from my current life as well as my past lives, and what I have remembered through my journey and connection to my soul. I hope that, by sharing my insights and understanding, you will open your heart and start your own journey to your truth.

The Earth is the soul's learning playground. At the soul level, we are all one, and nothing but pure love. I call it a soul, but you may call it God, or absolute consciousness, or whatever feels right to you. But the soul wants to have experiences, and in order to do so, it needs to have individuality. That is why human beings were created with free will. The soul wanted to experience what it was like to love and to be loved, to hurt someone and be hurt, to make and to destroy things, and every other possibility. One experience is not better or worse than another—they are just lessons.

Before we descend to Earth, we, along with our soul family, sign a contract to inhabit particular roles, so that we may learn specific lessons in our present lifetime. We take on different positions in different lifetimes—we may be a mother or father, sister or brother. We may be teachers or school bullies. Sometimes the reasons for coming to Earth are to provide lessons for others, like a young child who dies, forcing his or her parents to grow through this difficult lesson. We often wonder why our lives are the way they are, but the reality is that they are exactly what we intended before we came to Earth.

We do, however, have free will, so our actions can change the future. Certain events and people are set in our lives before we descend, but we still have the power to act in a manner that is right for us. Sometimes we must pay for the karma of our past lives, so even if we are living with honesty and goodness, unfortunate events may befall us. We still must atone for our old misbehavior. We can also say that the reverse is true. An undeserving person may get away with misdeeds, but he or she is creating karma that will catch up with that person in the next life. Clear your karma, and live in the best possible way that you can, so that you will be able to finish as many lessons as possible in this lifetime. Life is a mystery, but even if our human minds can't comprehend it, it is supposed to be the way it is.

Kyle told me that most people have seven lessons to learn in one human lifetime. If we finish all seven, then we get to learn another seven in the next lifetime. But if we only learn two, then we have to come back and not only finish learning the remaining five, but learn two new ones as well. Old souls have been to Earth thousands of times, and that's why they are able to navigate their lives more easily—they have learned many more lessons than a new soul.

When I look back at my life and that of my son, I am aware that we possessed deep knowing about what we needed to do in most situations. We remained calm no matter what hit us, and we were able to make rational decisions without much emotional distress. Without the many lessons we have learned in this life and past ones—and without the ability to carry this knowledge within us—we could not have been able to navigate our path with such certainty and accuracy.

Older souls are not necessarily better than newer ones. We cannot say that babies are less worthy than adults. New souls are simply on a different developmental level, and shouldn't be judged for this. It is more likely that difficult lessons will be handed to old souls, and simpler lessons to new souls. It is important for us to understand that one lesson is not more valuable than another—we are all, after all, on different paths, and the old souls have gone through the same learning process that the new souls are now experiencing.

Being human is an incredible honor and privilege, and

one should not waste the amazing opportunity it affords. As far as I know, Earth is the only place in the Universe where beings have free will, time, and physical bodies that allow them to accomplish anything they wish. It is up to each one of us to either make this planet a utopia, or destroy it. Throughout history, I don't think humans have ever been kind to the Earth. We have polluted its air, drilled into it, and extracted many natural resources from it, and we are overpopulating the land. It is time now—or never—to make changes for the better. Laneesh and Prishnah have spoken often about how they have seen many other civilizations destroy their planets because they haven't made the necessary changes in time.

One of my first meditation teachers used to say, "When you are dying in your hospital bed, there is only one question to ask yourself: *Did I love well?*" When we are born, we come with nothing, and we can't take anything with us when we leave this Earth. When we are on our deathbeds, we won't care how much money is in our accounts, or how many houses we own. The only thing we will be concerned with is whether the people we cared for knew how much we loved them.

Many humans become lost collecting material things. They think they will be happier if they have more money. And yes, money can be helpful, but all the money in the world cannot make us happy if we do not know how to love or how to share. It is possible, after all, to be wealthy but to have no heart. Generosity does not require wealth—it comes with kindness.

Some people collect knowledge. They study, acquire many diplomas, and believe that their intelligence makes them better—makes them special. But knowledge doesn't equate to wisdom. Wise men don't need to go to a university or have a formal education. Wise men know how to live fully. I would much rather be wise than learn formulas and facts that are not useful in loving someone.

Some people collect objects, and some collect people. They are addicted to buying things and adding more friends to their social circle. They are not happy without certain products, which is exactly what marketing professionals want people to feel. Or they update their social media profiles every 10 minutes, wanting to show others how well they are doing, when in reality, they may be feeling empty. I believe that many people engage in this sort of "collecting" so that they won't have to face their insecurities or the realities of their own lives. Material things cannot truly make a person happier. Pretending to be people we're not, and always seeking the approval of others, is tiring. We live in a world of duality, and we cannot always have what we want: happy, easy, wonderful times. Life can be boring, difficult, and sad. We are not really living if we are avoiding any of these aspects of our lives. In my life, I have experienced highs of love and joy shared with my family members and my children and the excitement of building my own business. I have also experienced the lows of boredom, sadness, and helplessness over loss of relatives and other loved ones and because of my divorce; and I've been able to tolerate intense spiritual transformation and emerge with insight and purpose.

Collecting power can be one of the most dangerous acts a person can engage in, as power can be used in the wrong ways. For centuries, humans have fought, trying to attain control over religions, land, and wealth. So many lives have been lost through these wars. These power struggles occur everywhere we look—countries trying to conquer other countries, companies trying to become the most powerful through competing with other companies, and even parents struggling with children and partners at odds with one another.

It is fine to collect things. It is wonderful to have money. It is useful to have knowledge. It is nice to have a large circle of friends. But the question becomes, what are we going to do with these things? Collecting can create a false sense of security, and it is time that we wake up from this illusion. The answer—the truth—is that by sharing our gifts with others and the Earth, we will attain the highest satisfaction possible. If you have money or knowledge, share it with the people who need it. If you look at the world from the perspective of the soul, all humans are created equal, and everyone on Earth is you. It is time for us to wake up from our dream that we are separate.

Many people ask Kyle and me how they can be more spiritual, believing that if they are spiritual, they will have all the answers. This is not the case. A person can meditate and channel beings, but this does not mean that that person is better or worse than anyone else. It is only when they use their gifts, and give them to others, that they can become spiritual and make a difference in this world. These gifts may include sharing knowledge, living the right way with your values, or even being true to one's self.

To me, being spiritual means being true to myself. A person's essence or core is nothing but love, so being spiritual necessarily means being loving. Love is the most important thing on Earth, and it gives us all great joy to live and share with others. People sometimes confuse being spiritual with being awakened. We can be awakened and understand the mysteries of life, but that does not mean we are spiritual, for we may still be living in arrogance and heartlessness. I have never understood why awakened beings want to be gurus who are worshipped. If we are one at the core, then there should be no such separation. We are attracted to wise beings because we see ourselves in them. And it is not worth being awoken if one cannot be loving and surrender to our oneness.

I believe that one of the soul's main goals while on Earth is to find a way of being whole, and remembering that our essence is love. In order to do this, a person must work on all aspects of his or her potential. One's emotions, intellectual development, spiritual awakening, and physical health are all equally important. For me, these four parts work together. If one is missing, I feel unbalanced. It is essential that attention be given to each of these facets and that one is not elevated above the others.

Many people also ask Kyle and me if they should meditate. Practicing meditation does not necessarily mean a person is spiritual. After all, maybe it is not your soul's purpose to meditate in this lifetime. I have known many people who do yoga and meditate daily but are far from spiritual. In a way, it is worse because they believe that they are automatically spiritual as a result of engaging in these practices. The truth is that I meditate because it is how I connect to my soul, but this is not the case for everyone.

Some may connect to their souls through cooking, gardening, or hiking in nature. Some may feel the strongest connection when they are painting or singing. The important thing is to find what your soul craves, and do that thing often. One thing isn't better than any other, but we must let go of our ego, which may try and convince us otherwise. I wish I could connect to my soul through singing or dancing—these would be much more fun than simply sitting around, meditating. But when I am meditating, I don't feel the need to sit for a set amount of time in order to stay connected. As I've probably meditated in several of my lifetimes, I may simply sit for five minutes one day and then not do so again for another few days. Every day, however, I do stop and breathe in order to feel connected to everything. For me, this takes 10 seconds. I also try to be kind to everyone I meet, treating people as I'd like to be treated—as if they were my family.

Many people also confuse spirituality with religion. I believe that both Buddha and Jesus Christ were awoken, and that they taught humans how to live the way they should. They didn't tell us to chant, or sing, or praise them as gods. They didn't command us to meditate for set periods of time, or to attend church in order to be awoken. To me, religion is nothing more than human beings' attempt to control others by using the teachings of the awakened in the wrong way, and for personal gain. It is fine to believe in any religion or system of belief. We have free will. But, I assure you, thousands of years ago wise men never instructed people to kill for their beliefs, nor did they punish those who didn't follow what they'd said. It is time for us to wake up and stop believing in false representations of God. If God is nothing but love, and we are connected to all things, then we are all God.

Many humans become lost in a state of drama, and this is especially a problem in the United States. Drama gives people an adrenaline rush, and they come to believe that they need such excitement in order to feel alive. But in reality, drama not only steals one's time and energy and causes a person's heart to shut down—it also results in that person hurting others. People who are addicted to drama become so used to it that they are afraid of letting it go. We do not, however, have to continue doing things in our lives that we don't want to do. Another mistake humans make is trying to change others instead of themselves. Some people spend a lifetime trying to do this, but the fact is it's hard enough controlling oneself—controlling others is impossible.

Most people do not live in the present. They are either dwelling in the past or projecting their future, and they do not exist in the here and now. But the past is gone, and the future has not arrived. We only have the present—each moment that is new, and now, and here. We need to be awakened and to stay in the moment, live in the moment, and love in the moment. This is when we are fully alive. And this is the best gift we can give to ourselves and to others.

Many humans are paralyzed by fear, but fear is not a phenomenon of the present moment. It comes from past experiences and future worries, and it is not always real. Yes, fear can be useful and save us from getting hurt or from dangerous situations. But the type of fear I am referring to now is the fear of being unloved, or of losing something you think you cannot live without. The truth is, however, that nothing can break you unless you allow it to. You have the control and power within you, and it is time for you to own it.

A person's ego is another potential obstacle. The voice in your head, for example, may be nothing other than your own self-importance trying to take control. It will tell you that you are not loved and that you need to do certain things in order to be so. It is lying—that's what your ego does. You need to stop trusting what your head is saying and begin listening to your heart. That is where your soul resides. Many humans never learned how to live from the heart, yet it is so much stronger and can spread so much more light than the mind. The heart knows love and knows how to show it to you and to others.

Loving yourself is the first step toward improving your life. You cannot truly love others if you don't know how to love yourself. What I would like each of you who are reading this book to do is repeat to yourself the following every morning for 30 days: "I love you, you are enough, and I am going to protect you." If you don't believe this after 30 days, keep repeating it. You may be looking to others for approval, but in reality you can give this to yourself. Remember that you are loved, you are love, and you are loving. You are enough. Forgive yourself for everything you have done, because you did the best that you could. You may have regrets, but you cannot change the past. We only have now, and we can change the future. This is our birthright, which you need to feel deeply in your heart.

You do not have to be spiritual in order to make a difference in this world. It is not a prerequisite for being a good citizen. Many people wrongly believe that they are powerless and have nothing to contribute. But in reality, we all have so much more potential than we could ever possibly comprehend. We all can make a difference, simply by giving, individually, what we can.

To contribute to the betterment of humanity and the Earth, we each need to do what we can in accordance with the evolution of our souls. What is most important is that, as individuals, we take responsibility. We can start with small, easy tasks, and then, if we find we can manage more, take on deeper, more difficult ones. I suggest that we each make a commitment to one task—one way in which we can make Earth an easier, better place to live—and do it as often as we can. It could be something as small as smiling at someone you don't know at least once a day. The next step could be offering to help someone in need. If you're not a people person, you could pick up litter when you see it, etc. The bottom line is that if everyone did one nice thing every day, can you imagine the sort of transformation we'd see in a short period of time?

After living in the United States for the last 20 years, I have never understood why Americans are most unkind to the people they are closest to. They treat their neighbors—or even strangers—with more kindness than their children or partners. This is something I still struggle to understand. I believe that the reality should be the opposite. We should be more caring, gentle, and loving to those who are dearest to us. It may be easier to love someone that you don't know— I've learned from firsthand experience that it is far more difficult to love those I've had to see on a daily basis, or experienced conflicts with. But this is a lesson for all: Take the high road, and be kind to the people who are closest to you, no matter how difficult it may be. Committing to this idea is the first step. As long as you hold on to this goal or intention and make small steps toward achieving it, that's all you can do. Don't expect things to change right away, but if you keep working at them, they will. This journey toward kindness will become easier, and you will be able to share your love with those closest to you.

Maybe you could say, "I love you," to your spouse, instead of "I hate you." Or you could find something positive to praise in your children, rather than drawing attention to their faults. You could spend more time with your family, or call your parents more often. You could make a point of saying thank-you whenever someone does something nice for you, or greet the people you meet in an elevator. Tell people you're sorry when you've done something wrong, or call someone you haven't spoken to in a while and let them know that you missed them.

Forgive someone you'd decided you'd never forgive in this lifetime. If you live from the heart, doing all this will not be difficult. And if people commit to these principles, small gestures such as these can go a long way.

Again, no judgment please. The heavy feeling of judgment is a burden our egos confer upon us and especially on our hearts. Do not judge yourself. After you have mastered this, you will find it easier not to judge others. If you miss completing your task or commitment one day, or if you get upset and yell at your child, remember that it is OK. Forgive yourself, and try and do better the next day. You have to be kind to yourself first, and then you can give that gift to others.

You can meditate and send your warm thoughts to other beings and to the Earth. You can bake or cook, and share what you've made with your neighbor. If time allows, you can volunteer at a school, shelter, or hospital. You can donate your old clothes and other items that you no longer need or use. If you are lucky enough to be in a position to, you can donate money to good causes. If you own a company, perhaps you could hire an extra person if you are able to. Try to come up with products that could help the Earth or humanity. There are endless ways to help others and to make contributions.

Be kind to everyone you meet. Treat everyone the way you would want to be treated. There are 7.6 billion people on this Earth—can you imagine the sort of change we can occasion if even a small portion of us committed to making a small difference every day?

Chapter 13 Reflections

I believe that first step to change this world is for each one of us to be a little kinder. We have to be kind to ourselves first and share that gift with others. The immense power of kindness can heal any scars in a heart as well as disease. We all have a choice to make. Now is the only time we have, and your commitment can go a long way, even if you haven't done actual work yet. Remember that the power of intention can change the whole energy of this Earth immediately. I hope you will join me to commit to be kind and share that gift with others so we can create a safer world.

What are the three things you can do to be kind to yourself?

1._____
_____
2._____
_____
3._____
_____

What are the three things you can do to be kind to others?

1._____
_____
2._____
_____
3._____
_____

Close your eyes, and take a deep breath. Open your eyes, and read the questions and the answers you have given. Take another deep breath, and tell yourself, "I am a kind person, and I am going to share that gift with others." Take another deep breath, and close your eyes. Imagine that you are being kind to yourself and others on different occasions and see people's smiling faces. When you open your eyes, remember how you felt when you were kind to yourself and others.

Can you make a small commitment to do something daily to make a difference in this world?

_____
_____

CHAPTER 14

My Dreams, Wishes, and Hopes

All human beings are also dream beings.
Dreaming ties all mankind together.
— Jack Kerouac

I want to share my deepest hopes, wishes, and dreams. These thoughts have emerged from my experiences as a daughter, immigrant, businesswoman, mother, lover, and fellow human being. I have come up with these ideas through my meditations, common life experiences, connection to my soul, and working with my angels. I am a big dreamer, but I believe we can accomplish great things if enough people on this Earth make a commitment to make their wishes, hopes, and dreams happen.

I have many dreams for the Earth and for humanity—the biggest is that all the beings on this planet will awaken and coexist in harmony. It is my dream that they will live from their hearts, feeling connected to everything, knowing and inhabiting the love that is the core of our beings. This will not be an easy road, I know. We have fallen so far off the path, and for so long. But many humans are realizing that we have gone astray and that we need to change. We have started to walk the path of atonement.

Some of my wishes and hopes are more realistic than others, but I have learned that the key to accomplishing something is first knowing what you want. I also know that setting an intention is more powerful than anyone could ever comprehend. So here I openly state what I would like to see happen in my lifetime. May these wishes come true, and may all of you who are reading this dream big and set your intentions high. Believe in yourself, as you are more powerful than you could ever imagine.

I wish that humans will make Earth a safe place to live:

I hope no one on this Earth will go to sleep hungry.

I hope all humans will have shelter, clean water, and education.

I hope all humans will realize that Earth is a living being, and that we must take good care of her.

I hope all humans will speak only what is helpful and truthful.

I hope all humans will be kind to each other and to themselves.

I hope all humans will have strong family ties.

I hope all humans will rely more on personal connections and less on technology, which makes people separate.

I hope all humans will spend more time in nature.

I hope all humans will feel their emotions fully.

MY DREAMS, WISHES, AND HOPES

I hope all humans will realize and enjoy the beauty of the Earth.

I hope all humans will treat the Earth and its animals, plants, and minerals with respect.

I hope all humans will stop judging themselves and others.

I hope all humans will take responsibility for their actions.

I hope all humans will realize that we cannot overpopulate the Earth.

I hope no child will be abused.

I hope there will be no more wars.

I hope there will be no more violence.

I hope there will be no power struggles, lies, or manipulations.

I hope all humans will treat each other with equality.

I hope all humans will accept and embrace each other's differences.

I hope all humans will learn to share.

I hope all humans will learn to forgive.

I hope there will be no more poverty.

I hope all humans will find jobs they enjoy performing.

I hope all humans will follow their hearts.

I wish for all humans to awaken and remember who they are:

I hope all humans will realize that they are enough and that they are loved.

I hope all humans will feel connected to love, to the Creator, and to themselves, rather than disconnected and alone.

I hope all humans will learn more of their lessons through joy and happiness, and less through sorrow, suffering, and pain.

I hope all humans will realize that they have free will to change anything they want in their lives.

I hope all humans will see the beauty they possess within themselves.

I hope all humans will find peace in their hearts.

I hope all humans will take back their individual power.

I hope all humans will remember that they have the ability to heal themselves.

I hope all humans will find their life's purpose.

I hope all humans will learn to slow down, breathe, and live in the present.

I hope all humans will let go of their egos and their unnecessary fears, and learn to trust again.

I hope all humans will realize that they are one and the same, and not become lost in the false identities of race, sex, religion, and political divides.

I hope all humans will realize that it was their choice to be on this planet.

I wish that new technology and information will be available to benefit humanity and the Earth:

I hope that alternative and free energy will become available, so that we will no longer take from Mother Earth.

I hope that this planet will be healed from all damage and misuse humans have inflicted upon it in the past.

I hope that we will find a solution to global warming.

I hope that cures for diseases will be found.

I hope that new crops will end world hunger.

Chapter 14 Reflections

The power of intentions is one of the strongest forces in existence along with love, truth, and kindness. Throughout this book, I've tried to cultivate all the qualities you have in yourself that you didn't know you had. You are ready to be a citizen of new world. We all want the same goal—for all humans to be happy, to be safe, and to be cared for. We want our Earth to be healthy and vibrant. We can live in harmony when each of us is committed to work toward the same goal. Let your voice be heard, set your intentions high, and let your dreams and wishes come true.

What are your personal dreams and wishes for yourself and your family?

1._____
_____
2._____
_____
3._____
_____

What are your dreams and wishes for your community, your country, and globally?

1._____
_____
2._____
_____
3._____
_____

What are your dreams and wishes for the Earth, all humans, and all beings in the Universe?

1._____
_____
2._____
_____
3._____
_____

Close your eyes, and take a deep breath. Open your eyes, and read the questions and the answers you have given. Take another deep breath, and imagine all your dreams and wishes have come true. Take another deep breath and close your eyes. Imagine how you would feel when all your dreams and wishes come true. When you open your eyes, remember how you felt when all your dreams and wishes came true.

CHAPTER 15

My Questions

*Nothing is impossible, the word itself says,
"I'm possible!"* – Audrey Hepburn

I am deeply concerned about the future of Earth and of humanity, so I asked Prishnah, Novysha, Kyrah, and Laneesh for their answers to my urgent questions.

Question: What is going to happen to Earth if we don't change anything?

Prishnah: The path that Earth is on right now is one of destruction. Unless we change the direction we are heading in, we have a very limited amount of time and resources.

Novysha: Human resources are running out as we speak, and there are so few life-sustaining planets within our reach that we have to find other ways of doing things, and we must slow down.

Kyrah: There are so many extinct animals and plants that we will never see again, all because of the choices humans have made. The holes in the ozone layer have sparked a chain reaction in our energy fields, causing a loss in our ability to protect ourselves from outside forces.

Laneesh: What is now happening to Earth is exactly the same thing that happened to many other planets that are no longer in existence. Even the time doors I use are getting weaker, making it harder to effect changes until enough positive energy is built back up on Earth. The situation is only getting worse.

Question: How and why did humans get to this point?

P: It was bound to happen because of males' egos and males' need to attain power. Because the soul is very stubborn, even though it knows it made a mistake, it still chooses to take the path in front of it instead of turning around.

N: I agree with Prishnah's answer, and, because of males' power struggles with themselves and others, we have gotten to a place where it is very hard to see the true light.

K: I don't want to spend my time talking about how we got here. What's important is how to get out of here.

L: Everything went wrong because there was no communication.

Question: Why me?

P: Earth is at the end of a giant cycle, which it will not be able to return from. It is heading toward ruin and disaster. You are one of only a few capable beings who can decipher and carry the information needed to change the direction the planet is going in. You can do this through sharing the information.

N: Only someone with female or mother energy can

carry all the information that is needed, and be able to understand it and put it into action.

K: You have the ability to see, to make the planet green again, and to help it breathe.

L: You carry the rare gift of being able to be physically in two places or more at the same time, and to be conscious of it all.

Question: Can I bring to humanity cures for diseases that are not available at this point?

P: You can definitely cure things, and also relay information about diseases and plagues.

N: You can also inspire people to open the doors within themselves in order to bring forth the information that already exists there.

K: Humans have a natural ability to heal themselves. You are going to reawaken that ability, which they have forgotten.

L: Yes. You have the access to all the information.

Question: Can I stop the extinction or eradication of natural resources?

P: You are going to give the information that will begin the long process of replenishing natural resources. You are going to introduce very simple processes, which can spread very fast.

N: You can—by teaching humans how to communicate with one other and with the planet, and how to listen and learn.

K: People have to learn to give and take.

L: Humans need to let go of some of their technology and go back to some of the older, more sensible ways.

Question: How can I awaken people?

P: By sharing the information that exists within you about the many planets that have gone down the same path our planet is heading. The truth will always awaken people.

N: You carry a natural ability to open the doors and windows inside people's souls, helping them to see the truth of their own situations. That is the gift that comes within your soul.

K: By making people slow down, stop looking, and listen.

L: By sharing the truth, even though it might be drastic, from a place of nonjudgmental clarity.

Question: Who are you?

P: We have been called many names. Some have called us angels, some aliens, and some spirits or entities. Others have called us teachers and guides, and others family and friends. What you need to know is that we are here to help you. That is our purpose.

N: We all agree with Prishnah. I would add sisters and mothers, but one thing you need to know about us from our souls—yes, we have souls, too—is that we are just here to save you from things that we know are coming.

K: We are all a part of the Greater Federation of Light—humans and us.

L: The other reason why we are coming so forcefully at this time is that human beings are finally at the level, and possess the technology, to be able to save themselves.

Question: What can humans do to change Earth's future?
P: Take a moment each day and align themselves to the cosmic energy, so that they are looking at positive solutions to things all the time.

N: Focus on doing something positive each day that leads them to know the other people in the community. Random acts seldom go unnoticed, and are quite addictive.

K: Take a daily walk in the heart of nature. If they can't go for a walk in nature, then they should sit in a park, and feel that they are a part of the whole. People are so disconnected, and so used to being alone, that it will take some effort for them to connect with everyone and everything.

L: A lot of stuff can be changed through using our minds. This is a little challenging, but I want you to think of something that you have done wrong. In your mind, go back to the time you did it, and do it differently in your mind this time. That will change the energy rapidly.

Question: What are the specific roles or talents you share when you send a healing?
P: I am the cognitive force of the three, and I work on people's thought patterns.

N: The physical is my area, so I work on physiology and can bring healing to the body.

K: I deal with the affective elements and therefore focus on emotional healing.

L: I don't do healing.

Question: What are the special gifts you are going to share with us to help humanity and the Earth?

P: I carry the knowledge that can help the world overcome obstacles.

N: I work with the energy of the light to brighten the dark spots on this planet.

K: I bring the element of love and hope to the world.

L: I am here to help Ariyana travel to the future and return, carrying the information needed to change the path this planet is going down.

Question: Can you give us your wishes for our future?

P: My wish is that you will turn your world around, and learn to trust yourself, which will give you the ability to trust others around you. The only reason we are here is in the hope that you won't make the same mistakes that we have made. The main mistake was waiting too long.

N: My belief is that happiness and joy can make for a very pleasant place to be. So I wish happiness and joy to everyone. If you carry happiness and joy, they will create love within your soul, which we all know is one of the strongest emotions. This would put us on the fast track.

K: I will give everyone a diamond, as diamonds carry the energy of clarity and truth. I will ask everyone to keep his or her diamond cleared, so that conscious and unconscious will work together. That's how I will change the world.

L: How can you be kind to others if you are not kind to yourself? My wish is happiness and love to everyone in the past, present, and future.

Chapter 15 Reflections

I believe in the power of collectiveness. One person cannot move a mountain, but if enough of us get together and work toward the same goal, the potential is limitless. I have my unique gifts, which I am committed to use for the betterment of all. I hope all of you will join me to make a difference for the future of humanity, Earth, and the whole Universe. All I ask is for you to commit and keep doing something to make a difference every day, no matter how small it is. If you are fortunate and have the power to make a bigger difference, then I hope you will do the best you can. Our future depends on us. Let's make a brighter future for ourselves and for our children.

What have you learned from this book?

1. _____
_____
2. _____
_____
3. _____
_____

What changes are you going to make after reading this book?

1._____

2._____

3._____

What changes do you want to see happen in your lifetime?

1._____

2._____

3._____

Please visit my website, www.astarchild.com. There will be messages from my star family, and you can listen to activations and meditations. Your support is crucial for the immediate and drastic changes we need to make. Thank you very much for reading my book, and I wish you love, peace, and happiness.

ACKNOWLEDGMENTS

First and foremost, I want to thank Kyle Matthews for his guidance, support, and friendship while I was realizing who I was and writing this book. Without his ability to communicate with multidimensional beings, this book wouldn't have been born. I am eternally grateful for his presence in my life. He is one of my guardian angels on Earth.

I also want to send gratitude and love to my little sister, Akiko. She has always supported me, trusted me, and loved me unconditionally. She is my best friend, and I am very lucky to have her in my life.

I want to thank my family on Earth: my mother and father for showing me that the world is a safe place, and my children, who have no idea how much joy they bring into my life. Without my children, I would have lost the hope and light that kept me going.

And to my cosmic family, thank you for your love and trust in me. I look forward to working with you and making a difference through our service to humanity and to Earth.

My gratitude flows abundantly to Cary Granat, my dear friend, who has been one of the guardians of this project and who gave me continual faith and support.

I owe much gratitude to my wonderful book agents Rick

Richter and Lane Zachary at Zachary Shuster Harmsworth. Their advice and guidance were most useful and valuable for a first-time author. Thank you both for your wisdom and experience; without you, I would have been lost.

A big thank-you goes to my amazing editor, Bruce Wexler. You have helped my writing, clarifying my points and making my book better and more powerful. I was very lucky to be able to work with you.

David Wilk and his team have worked on my book production tirelessly and came up with beautiful designs, layout and finishing touches. It was a joy to work with such talented and professional people.

I want to thank everyone who has touched my heart so far—strangers and friends alike. I owe much gratitude to all the healers and psychics who have shared their gifts with me. I want to send special thanks to all the therapists and body workers who, day and night, took care of my physical needs. I would also like to recognize those who helped me with my furniture business, my home, and my children—I couldn't have done what I did without your hard work. I am here today because of each and every one of you.

ABOUT THE AUTHOR

Ariyana was born and raised in Tokyo, Japan. She moved to the United States at the age of 18 to attend the University of Southern California. It was there that she met her ex-husband, with whom she built a multimillion-dollar furniture business from scratch. After a series of revelations through meditation, and with the help of psychics and healers, Ariyana connected with her life's purpose. She quit her position as the president of the furniture company, and, with the help of her cosmic family, has become a healer and consultant. She lives in Los Angeles, with her two children.

For more information on her work, visit:
www.astarchild.com.

MAY 5 - 2015